SIDE BY SIDE

SIDE BY SIDE

Integrated Neighborhoods in America

By
Norman M. Bradburn,
Seymour Sudman, *and*
Galen L. Gockel
with the assistance of
Joseph R. Noel

QUADRANGLE BOOKS   *Chicago 1971*

Library of Congress Catalog Card Number: 75-143570
SBN 8129-0186-X

The research reported herein was supported by Public Health Service
Grants 5-RO1-MH12381-01, 5-RO1-MH12381-02, and 5-RO1-
MH12381-03 from the National Institute of Mental Health.

An earlier version of Chapter 3 and the Appendix appeared in *The
Journal of Business of the University of Chicago* (Vol. 42, No. 1.
January, 1969) as "The Extent of Racially Integrated Housing in the
United States" by Seymour Sudman, Norman M. Bradburn, and
Galen L. Gockel. Permission for use granted by The University of
Chicago Press © 1969 by The University of Chicago.

Preface

THE RESEARCH reported in this book originated in the personal experiences of the authors. In 1965 we were all living in racially integrated neighborhoods in Chicago and were active in our respective local community organizations. We were frequently asked by our neighbors to apply the findings of social science to help keep our neighborhoods stable. A survey of literature yielded some insights, but there was disappointingly little in the way of systematic research. There had been several studies of changing neighborhoods, but they provided little encouragement. We thus began to think about a study that would be a more systematic survey of racially integrated neighborhoods in the United States, and might, if we were successful, give a better understanding of the characteristics and problems of integrated neighborhoods.

At a series of National Opinion Research Center seminars, the possibility of a national study of integrated neighborhoods was explored. There was much interest, but also some doubts about the feasibility of the study. The principal questions raised were whether it was possible to define a neighborhood and whether there were enough integrated neighborhoods to make a national study worthwhile.

With the help of a Ford Foundation faculty research grant from the Graduate School of Business of the University of Chicago, we were able to conduct a pilot study in three cities—Washington, D.C., Atlanta, Georgia, and San Jose, California. The results of this pilot study (Sudman and Bradburn, 1966) were encouraging. With these results available, we applied for and received a grant from the National Institute of Mental Health for the first national study of integrated neighborhoods. This study was conducted in the spring of 1967.

Now, after the long delay that accompanies most such studies, here are some of the basic results of our efforts. These findings, as well as others not included in this book, are presented in greater detail in a research monograph, *Racial Integration in American Neighborhoods: A Comparative Survey* (NORC Report No. 111-B), by the same authors.

As our readers and we are well aware, there have been changes in attitudes toward integration between 1965 and 1970, and even between 1967 and now. These changes in attitudes are probably greater among blacks than among whites, and perhaps now run more in the direction of racial separation rather than integration, although the evidence that basic attitudes have changed is meager at best. We believe, however, that our findings and predictions are still essentially valid.

The study reported on here is primarily one of whites' willingness to live in racially integrated neighborhoods. As the study shows, blacks live in integrated neighborhoods for reasons related to the quality of housing and the neighborhood, rather than because they want to socialize with whites. The degree of socializing between races was so low in 1967 that it is hardly possible to reduce it further.

We would expect that the situation will change through time, and hope, if funds are available, to conduct a follow-up study in the next few years on what has happened since 1967. Doubtless, the results of that study will also be a couple of years out of date by the time they are published.

Some of our readers may be disappointed that this is not a comprehensive study of black housing or of black attitudes toward integration but instead deals mainly with black and white families with relatively high incomes in middle-class neighborhoods. We can only reply that we were not able to study all aspects of housing choice for the entire population and that the study design is very complex as it is. We believe that our study represents an important departure from that of the usual cross-sectional study of the population and, as such, sheds some new light on the problem of housing choice for both black and white Americans. If we are to be criticized, we hope it is for what we have done, rather than for what we have not been able to include.

NORMAN M. BRADBURN

SEYMOUR SUDMAN

GALEN L. GOCKEL

December, 1970

Acknowledgments

THOUSANDS OF individuals were involved in this research. Acknowledgments must first be made to the interviewers on the National Opinion Research Center's national staff who located the integrated neighborhoods in their communities, participated in the sampling procedures, and conducted almost 8,500 interviews. Celia Homans, assisted by Gwen Houston, supervised these efforts with great skill and sensitivity during a field period that extended for a full year. Our greatest debt of gratitude is to the 3,500 city informants, the 1,200 community leaders, and the more than 3,800 households who provided us with the data.

The thousands of questionnaires we accumulated were coded under the able supervision of Frances Harris. Solutions to complex data-processing problems and expert advice were provided by Earl D. Main and Frank Schilling of NORC's data-processing staff. Judson Lawrie undertook the laborious task of writing the necessary recoding and control card instructions.

During the study's developmental period, ideas and suggestions were obtained from Jacob J. Feldman, Frederick

Mosteller, Neil Gold, Eunice and George Grier, Robin Williams, and Brian Berry. Within NORC at that time, Robert L. Crain, John W. C. Johnstone, James J. Vanecko, Eva Weinberg, and Peter H. Rossi gave their valuable advice as the study was being planned.

The first manuscript draft was reviewed by Rossi, James H. Lorie, and Harold Baron. Joseph R. Noel and Carlyn J. K. Rottsolk served as research assistants, and part of Chapter 11 was written by Noel.

The full version of the manuscript, which was published by NORC as a research report in 1970, was edited by Mary A. Spaeth, with the assistance of Elaine Richardson. The grueling task of typing the many versions of the manuscript was accomplished by the NORC Steno Pool under the supervision of Toshi Takahashi. Special thanks go to Nancy Nagel, who typed the bulk of the manuscript twice.

Lastly, this version of the report would not exist had it not been for the encouragement of Oscar Cohen of the Anti-Defamation League of B'nai B'rith and the assistance of Ivan Dee of Quadrangle Books, who handled the challenging task of editing and paring down the original manuscript into its present form.

N. M. B.

S. S.

G. L. G.

Contents

SIDE BY SIDE

1 *Introduction*

FAMILIES LIVE in neighborhoods, and the character of those neighborhoods determines in large part the kinds of personal relationships, jobs, and community facilities that are available to them. A person denied the right to live where he chooses because of his race is also denied the right to participate fully in the opportunities for economic and personal growth offered by society. The purpose of this report is to investigate the characteristics of racially integrated neighborhoods in an attempt to discover whether and under what conditions Negroes and whites can live together.

Although the problem of discrimination in housing has been a major concern to many for a long time, there is remarkably little comprehensive information—systematically gathered and organized—on the extent of interracial housing or on how a stably integrated neighborhood differs from a racially changing neighborhood. Using census data, the Taeubers (1965) showed that, even though there has been some reduction in racial segregation in U.S. cities (at least as measured by a statistical segregation index), the cities remain segregated. Their study, however, was limited to overall trends—the data they used precluded any investigation of the factors that influence stability or change at the neighborhood level.

The most extensive series of reports on particular neighborhoods were those prepared for the Comm ission on Race and Housing. While these studies are extremely valuable in detailing the experiences of a substantial number of neighborhoods, they were done in the mid-1950s and were primarily concerned with racially changing neighborhoods rather than with stably integrated ones.

The principal exception to this generalization is *Privately Developed Interracial Housing* (1960), Eunice and George Grier's study of new, privately developed, interracial housing based on interviews with builders conducted in 1955. The Griers' major achievement was locating and investigating a substantial number of integrated areas (50) and demonstrating that such areas could be successful. Unfortunately, they were not able to draw systematic samples or investigate differences between segregated and integrated neighborhoods.

To our knowledge, the national study reported in this book is the only one to use sample survey techniques directly to investigate the characteristics of integrated neighborhoods. The absence of other nationwide studies cannot be blamed on any lack of interest by social scientists. The real obstacle has been in finding the right—that is, integrated—neighborhoods to study.

THE DEFINITIONAL PROBLEM

What is an integrated neighborhood? Since there is no generally accepted definition of this term, any study of integrated neighborhoods—and most particularly one that attempts to be nationwide and systematic—must make extremely clear the way in which it is using the term.

This study has considered two possible definitions. The

first defines integration in terms of the "state" of a neighborhood, which is expressed as the proportion of Negroes
living in the neighborhood. If the proportion exceeds
some arbitrary percentage, such as 5, 10, or 20, or is approximately equal to the proportion of Negroes in the entire city or metropolitan area, the neighborhood is
classified as integrated.

A "state" definition allows one to describe integrated
neighborhoods comparatively. Comparisons may be made
in terms of percentages or in terms of the deviation of the
percentage of Negroes from that expected if the Negro
population of the city were equally distributed in each
neighborhood.

The advantage of the "state" definition of integration is
that it can be readily applied to cross-sectional statistical
data such as census data or data obtained by fairly simple
sample survey techniques. Such data are relatively easy to
obtain for comparisons among different places or across
different time periods. The definition has several concep-
tual disadvantages, however, that tend to obscure the social
processes taking place in integrated neighborhoods. For
example, it obscures the differences between integrated
neighborhoods and changing neighborhoods in the short
run. This definition also forces one to say that neighborhoods are becoming more integrated up to a certain
point, and then, as the proportion of Negro residents
increases, to say that they are on their way to becoming
resegregated.

The alternative definition focuses on the "process" of integration rather than the "state" or proportion of integration. The "process" definition considers not only the current racial composition of the neighborhood but, more im-
portantly, the racial composition of those who are moving
into the neighborhood. The critical variable is the neighborhood's openness to both Negro and white potential residents. The fact that both whites and Negroes can move,
and are moving, into a neighborhood makes it, by defini-

tion, integrated. Thus, a neighborhood that is 50 percent white (or even 90 percent white) would not be considered integrated if no new white families were moving in, because eventually it would become all Negro. Instead, the neighborhood would be considered changing. The "process" definition also would exclude predominantly white areas with a few Negro families if no more Negro families were allowed in. A neighborhood with a quota system that permitted new white and Negro residents in some definite ratio would, however, be considered integrated.

With the use of a "process" definition of integration, which concentrates on the racial mixture of incoming residents, the question of the overall proportion of Negroes in a neighborhood becomes a separate problem. Similarly, integrated neighborhoods, again as opposed to racially changing ones, that have differing proportions of Negroes and whites are also worthy of study. Under the "process" definition, of course, changing neighborhoods are considered segregated, regardless of the relative proportions of white and Negro residents.

Although it is less commonly used, the "process" definition seems the appropriate one to use because it embodies the central question of discrimination in housing: that is, whether people are being denied access to housing opportunities simply because of their race. We feel that the "state" definition causes confusion between the issue of the current proportion of Negroes and whites living together in an area and the freedom-of-access question regarding whether both Negroes and whites can move into an area.

The critical reader might note that we included in our "process" definition the fact that both Negroes and whites can move, and *are* currently moving, into the area. One might say that the only relevant question is whether people *can* move into an area rather than whether they are actually doing so. While in theory there is some merit to this argument, it is difficult to evaluate claims of neighborhood informants that all-white neighborhoods are in fact open to potential. Negro residents when no Negroes are moving in. Since there are many ways in which potential Negro residents may be discouraged from moving into an all-white neighborhood, it would be exceedingly difficult to classify accurately all those neighborhoods that would in reality accept Negroes and those that would not. Thus we take what may seem a conservative approach, requiring that in order for a predominantly white neighborhood to be integrated, some Negro families must have moved into it in the recent past and, in addition, there must be the serious expectation that other Negro families will be moving into it in the near future. On the other hand, there may be those who feel that we are taking too liberal a position by not requiring that a specific proportion of the new residents in a white neighborhood be Negro.

Some important qualifications to the "process" definition must be pointed out. In some southern cities Negroes and whites live in close proximity, and both Negroes and whites continue to move in and out. The value of the Negro housing is, however, generally far below that of the whites. These areas, therefore, cannot be considered integrated. Conversely, in some northern cities Negroes and whites live on adjacent blocks in comparable housing, but not next door to each other. As long as the neighborhoods are not changing, even though the Negro and white families may have little or no social contact with one another, they qualify as integrated under the "process" definition. These two qualifications sharpen the boundaries of the "process" definition by stressing the willingness and ability of both Negroes and whites to live *in close proximity in equal-quality housing*. The question of housing integration, however, is to be sharply differentiated from that of "social integration" among Negro and white families. Whether such social integration occurs in conjunction with housing integration is a separate question, one that we discuss in a later chapter.

TYPES OF INTEGRATED NEIGHBORHOODS

In the long run, all neighborhoods change, both in the types of housing they offer and in the kinds of residents they attract. Some of the stable integrated neighborhoods studied for this report may in time become all Negro or all white, and neighborhoods that are currently white or Negro segregated could become stably integrated. A stable integrated neighborhood is defined as one that neighborhood informants believed would continue to have both Negroes and whites moving in during the next five years. Conversely, those neighborhoods our informants thought would change, so that in five years only Negroes would be moving in, were classified as Negro segregated and not as integrated, despite the fact that some whites are currently moving in.

Defining neighborhoods as integrated does not mean that the neighborhoods form a homogeneous group. The proportion of Negroes moving into an area will be a crucial variable in determining the nature and effects of integrated living. For this reason we have subdivided our integrated neighborhoods into the following five types, which are based primarily on the proportion of Negroes living in a neighborhood:

Open—those with two or more Negro families but fewer than one percent Negro residents;

Moderately integrated—those with from one to ten percent Negro families;

Substantially integrated—those with more than ten percent Negro families;

Integrated in localities with very few Negroes—neighborhoods with some Negroes in localities where the proportion of Negroes is less than two percent and where there are no segregated Negro neighborhoods; and

Integrated rural areas—those primarily in the South where incorporated areas are segregated, but rural areas have been traditionally integrated.

RESEARCH PLAN

This study is concerned primarily with the first three types of integrated neighborhoods described above. We interviewed residents in these neighborhoods as well as residents in segregated neighborhoods that were specially chosen to match the characteristics of the integrated neighborhoods that we had selected.

We divided the research operations for the study into the following three phases:

Phase I—Collecting data that would enable us to draw a sample of integrated neighborhoods in the 73 primary sampling units (PSUs) used in the National Opinion Research Center's (NORC) national probability sampling frame (Johnstone and Rivera. 1965).

Phase II—Interviewing neighborhood leaders to obtain basic information about neighborhood characteristics. The interviews were conducted in 311 neighborhoods (230 integrated, 49 white segregated, and 32 Negro segregated) chosen from those identified in Phase I.

Phase III—Selecting a sample of households in most of the chosen neighborhoods and interviewing a member of each household drawn in the sampling.

We shall discuss each of these phases briefly. (A more detailed description of the research methodology is given in the Appendix.) In Phase I, begun and completed in the autumn of 1966, we identified geographical areas as neighborhoods and determined whether or not they were integrated. We ultimately had to have precise geographical boundaries for sampling purposes, so we began with the 17,000 census tracts that the NORC interviewers had classified as containing or not containing an integrated neighborhood. Since the NORC classifications were based on the 1960 census and, hence, were six years old, we could not use them to determine if both white and Negro families were currently moving into a neighborhood, or what neighborhoods were in a tract. They did, however, provide

a start, because, according to our definition, tracts containing both Negro and white households were potentially
integrated.

Next, our interviewers contacted possible sources of city-
wide information, such as officials in local human relations organizations; realtors; bankers; members of civic,
political, religious, housing, and educational groups; and
local newspapers. In all, 3,500 respondents were contacted.

The information collected in Phase I was reasonably accurate, but it was not expected to be (nor did it turn out to
be) perfect. Some of the people we interviewed gave information that was dated, some were confused, and some were
just not well enough informed. Errors made in the first
phase were corrected in the later phases.

The Phase I search located several thousand integrated
neighborhoods. Initially, we selected 200 of these neighborhoods for study and 100 control neighborhoods (50
white segregated and 50 Negro segregated) for comparison.[1] In Phase II we interviewed an average of four
leaders in each neighborhood to determine its characteristics. The leaders were selected from each of the
following groups:

1. *Religious*—the clergyman of the most active church
in the neighborhood;

2. *Educational*—the principal or PTA president of a
neighborhood school;

3. *Civic*—an officer or staff member of an active
community organization; and

4. *Real estate*—a realtor active in the neighborhood.

The results of these interviews will be discussed exten-
sively in later chapters. We concern ourselves here with

[1]The final number of neighborhoods was 311 because, occasionally, an area
originally identified in Phase I as one neighborhood, was, on the basis of
the Phase II informants' data, divided into two neighborhoods. Moreover,
some segregated neighborhoods were found to be integrated (and vice
versa); hence, the 50–50 split among control neighborhoods turned out to
be 49 white segregated and 32 Negro segregated.

the responses that were used for estimating the number of integrated neighborhoods.

Although we had expected some of our city-wide leaders to describe a neighborhood as integrated when it was not, and also to be unaware of some integrated areas, we found that they consistently underestimated the number of integrated neighborhoods. The reason for this underestimation was that they classified as Negro segregated (changing) some neighborhoods that local leaders and residents considered integrated because both Negroes and whites could move and were moving into them.

It is possible that in some cases the city-wide informants were correct and the neighborhood informants wrong about the stability of their individual neighborhoods; but, where we were able to check, the results mainly confirmed the judgments of the neighborhood informants. We analyzed the move-in dates of white and Negro residents in doubtful neighborhoods, and in most of these neighborhoods, a large percentage of whites had moved in during the few years preceding the study.

We also depended upon the neighborhood leaders to help us determine whether an area we had chosen to study was in fact a neighborhood and what its boundaries were. There was substantial agreement among the neighborhood informants on the neighborhood name, but somewhat less agreement on its exact boundaries. Where one informant was in considerable disagreement with the others on boundaries, additional interviews were conducted with other neighborhood leaders to reach a consensus. (Three areas where there was no consensus on boundaries and no common name were excluded from the study as not being valid neighborhoods.)

The Phase II interviews with the neighborhood informants were used to determine the final classification of neighborhoods as integrated or segregated. Ultimately, 30 neighborhoods that had been designated as segregated by the Phase I city-wide informants were reclassified as integrated, and 11 neighborhoods formerly described as integrated by Phase I informants were reclassified as segregated.

Phase III, conducted in the spring of 1967, consisted of interviews with a probability sample of about 4,000 households in the sample neighborhoods selected earlier. Within the household, any knowledgeable adult resident served as a respondent. Since most of the interview questions were about experiences relating to housing choice and living in the neighborhood, we did not feel that it was important to have an exact probability sample of individuals. Inevitably, then, we had more female respondents than male. Our conclusions about the characteristics of the neighborhood residents, the factors that determine housing choices, and life in integrated neighborhoods were based on the information the respondents gave us.

OVERVIEW OF FINDINGS

In this section we summarize briefly the major findings of the study that are presented in detail in the subsequent chapters.

In Chapter 2 we offer profiles of six neighborhoods that, it is hoped, will give the reader some general feeling for the range of integrated neighborhoods that we studied.

In Chapter 3 we present statistical estimates of the extent of integrated housing in the United States. On the basis of our data, we estimate that 36 million Americans, or 19 percent of the population, lived in racially integrated neighborhoods in the spring of 1967. The total number of households in integrated neighborhoods is estimated at 11 million. In the chapter itself, we break these figures down regionally.

In spite of the large number of integrated neighborhoods that we found, very few Negroes live in these neighborhoods. Thus, the average white resident of an integrated neighborhood lives in a community where he usually is in a very substantial majority. For example, of the estimated 11 million households found in integrated neighborhoods, only about 760,000, or about 7 percent, are Negro. Half of the households in integrated neighborhoods are in ones where Negroes account for 3 percent or less of the total population.

It is clear that the extent of Negro demand compared to white demand for housing is an extremely important factor in determining both the relative proportion of Negroes in the neighborhood and the relative rates of increase in Negro residents. Nonetheless, it is also clear from the data in Chapter 4 that, based on the history of integrated as well as of Negro segregated neighborhoods, a hostile response on the part of white residents is also connected with a rapid increase in Negro occupancy. In our view, Negro demand for housing plays a dual role in the process of integration. This demand has a direct effect on the proportion of Negroes moving into the neighborhood. It also has an indirect effect by provoking initial white hostility, which then leads to a greater white exodus.

Chapter 5 discusses differences in the demographic characteristics of residents in the various types of neighborhoods. Reflecting the disparity between Negro and white incomes in the country, we found that open neighborhoods have a median income that is higher and substantially integrated neighborhoods have a median income that is lower than the median income for all households in the United States. This difference between open and substantially integrated neighborhoods is just one of the many presented in this study which indicate that among all integrated neighborhoods the substantially integrated ones tend on the average to be "poorer" than the open and moderately integrated ones.

Although differences in general economic levels are the most apparent, there is also some evidence that greater religious, ethnic, economic, and educational variety is more characteristic of integrated neighborhoods than of white segregated ones. The data in Chapter 6, "Variety Is the Spice," clearly support the generally held view that white Americans prefer homogeneous neighborhoods; nevertheless, the same data also partially reflect a more general willingness on the part of whites in integrated neighborhoods to live among people of all kinds; at least the residents of integrated neighborhoods do not reject neighborhood diversity.

Chapter 7 examines the characteristics of housing in integrated neighborhoods, including such factors as size, market value or rent, and ownership. The data indicate clearly that, although there are more renters in integrated neighborhoods than in white segregated neighborhoods, the majority of white residents living in all kinds of integrated neighborhoods are homeowners. Only among Negroes in substantially integrated neighborhoods do renters constitute a majority of the residents.

In Chapter 8 the focus of attention shifts to the attitudes of neighborhood residents toward integration. Rather surprisingly, the attitudes of white residents have relatively little relationship to the type of neighborhood in which they live. White residents of open and moderately integrated neighborhoods tend to be more pro-integration, while white residents in substantially integrated neighborhoods are more anti-integration than those in white segregated neighborhoods. These differences, as the chapter shows, turn out to be due to variables other than residence in a particular type of neighborhood. Instead, the attitudes of whites are strongly related to the region of the country in which they live and their level of education.

The attitudes of Negro residents of integrated neighborhoods do show some differences according to the type of neighborhood in which they live. In general, Negroes who live in open and moderately integrated neighborhoods are more militant about civil rights and are more likely to have participated in civil rights activities than are Negroes who live in substantially integrated or Negro segregated neighborhoods.

In Chapters 9 through 11 we examine, in some detail, satisfaction with and participation in significant neighborhood institutions, such as schools, churches, and recreational facilities. Perhaps the most salient conclusion of these chapters is a negative one—that there is, in fact, very little systematic difference between integrated and segregated neighborhoods. We were impressed with the great variance among neighborhoods in their problems and in their good and bad points, but, overall, the fact that a neighborhood is integrated or segregated often makes very little difference.

School integration is the subject of Chapter 9. Although we expected that the proportion of residents who have children attending integrated schools and the proportion of Negro students in the schools would not be the same in all of the different types of neighborhoods we studied, we were impressed with the relatively small degree of differences we actually found. More impressive, however, was the fact that large proportions of residents in white segregated neighborhoods have children in integrated schools.

Ratings of the quality of neighborhood schools by both our neighborhood informants and the residents varied among neighborhood types. Schools in substantially integrated and Negro segregated neighborhoods were rated lower than schools in the other types of neighborhoods. These differences proved, however, to be almost entirely a function of the economic level of the neighborhood, with the poorer quality schools being in the poorer neighborhoods.

In addition, although schools were more commonly rated as positive features in white segregated neighborhoods than in any other type of neighborhood, analysis of the data suggests that schools play a significant role in the future stability of the neighborhood only in those substantially integrated neighborhoods where there is high Negro demand for housing. In these areas rapid change in the proportion of Negro students in the schools, or in the perceived quality of the schools, may precipitate a decline in white demand for housing and upset the stability of the neighborhood.

Chapter 10 shows that churches turn out to be much more segregated than schools. Indeed, churches may be the most segregated of the voluntary organizations in any of the neighborhoods. Integration in the churches does not follow the pattern of integration in the schools. While the proportion of Negro children in the schools is almost a direct function of the proportion of Negro families in the neighborhood, the proportion of integrated churches is inversely related to the proportion of Negro families. Where there are fairly substantial proportions of Negroes in the neighborhood, there is a tendency for Negro residents to attend an all-Negro church. This pattern has continued in integrated neighborhoods that have within them, or surrounding them, a sufficient Negro population to support a church.

Catholics are more likely to attend "interracial" churches, that is, ones in which, by our definition, both races are members and Negroes constitute two percent or more of the total. They are not, however, as favorably disposed to church integration as Protestants who attend interracial churches. We interpret these differences as reflecting the differing structures of the two churches. Protestants are more free to select a congregation that is sympathetic with their beliefs about integration, while Catholics are generally constrained to attend the church in the parish in which they reside. Although Catholic respondents are more likely than their Protestant neighbors to attend interracial churches, there is evidence suggesting that, for them, behavior precedes attitudes. Among whites, Catholics are less likely to say they are "pleased" that their churches are attended by both whites and Negroes, and are substantially less likely to report that whites and Negroes mingle at church affairs. It appears that for Catholics attendance at interracial churches is influenced by factors other than personal preference; a prime factor is undoubtedly the tradition of observing rather explicit parish boundaries.

In Chapter 11, "Happiness Is . . . ." we show that there are no differences among whites in the general satisfactions of living in integrated or segregated neighborhoods. Negroes who live in substantially integrated neighborhoods and were originally faced with hostile reactions by their neighbors upon moving in are least happy with their neighborhoods. On the other hand, Negroes in open or moderately integrated neighborhoods are generally quite happy with their neighborhoods. Chapter 11 also shows that there is an extremely small amount of social interaction between the races in integrated neighborhoods. Although there is some evidence of an increase in interracial neighboring as the proportion of Negroes in the neighborhood increases, the higher level of intra-racial, as compared with interracial, social contact is overwhelming.

In the final chapter, Chapter 12, we speculate about the future of integrated neighborhoods. In general, the people we interviewed apparently gave fairly realistic appraisals of the future of their neighborhoods. Both informants and residents in neighborhoods where there was a high Negro demand for housing reported that there would be substantial changes in the proportion of Negroes living in the neighborhoods within the next five years. Residents in these areas showed much more concern about their neighborhoods changing than residents in the areas where Negro demand for housing was low. They felt, nevertheless, that the neighborhoods would continue to be integrated—both Negroes and whites would be moving in—for at least five years. In all neighborhoods, renters were more concerned about their neighborhoods changing than homeowners were.

In the final portion of Chapter 12 we make predictions about the future of the white segregated neighborhoods during the next decade. We estimate that the proportion

of American households in integrated neighborhoods will
slowly rise to about 35 percent by 1980. While some currently integrated neighborhoods will become segregated
during this period, many of the presently segregated neighborhoods will become integrated. We expect modest
increases in the proportions of Negroes in open and moderately integrated neighborhoods, and a major increase in
substantially integrated neighborhoods in the North and
West. We anticipate, however, that the majority of the
neighborhoods in the country will continue to be white
segregated for the foreseeable future.

2 Neighborhood Profiles

IN THIS chapter we describe six of the 200 sample integrated neighborhoods studied for this report. We decided to profile these particular neighborhoods because they represent broad classes of currently integrated communities in the United States. By describing the neighborhoods, we hope to show how the use of the "process" definition of integrated worked to uncover many neighborhoods that might otherwise not have been included in a study of integrated neighborhoods. To qualify as integrated, a neighborhood must still have been attracting both white and Negro residents. Through the application of this definition, we found that, in the average integrated neighborhood, only three percent of the population was Negro. Thus, the fact that the majority of the integrated communities profiled here are overwhelmingly white should come as no surprise.

Another reason for providing profiles of these particular neighborhoods at this point is to add flesh and blood to the bare statistical bones that comprise much of the material in subsequent chapters of this book. Although percentages

19

and averages are necessary tools for summarizing research data, they cannot be expected to convey the subtleties that distinguish the various neighborhoods from each other. Each community we studied possesses an individuality of its own, each is peopled by real families, and each is subject to unique influences both from within and outside its boundaries.

Our descriptions of these neighborhoods are based primarily on the information we received from the neighborhoods' own leading citizens—school officials, clergymen, members of civic organizations, and realtors—four of whom were interviewed in each neighborhood. We asked these neighborhood informants to tell us as much as they could about their neighborhood, and in particular how white residents responded to desegregation. We also asked them to predict the future status of integration in their neighborhood. Moreover, when possible we also talked with the first Negroes who had moved into these neighborhoods about the neighborhood's response to desegregation and about current racial relationships.

Feeling that neighborhoods, as well as individuals, should be guaranteed confidentiality in research reports, we have disguised all names of the communities and towns described in the pages that follow. Occasionally it has been necessary to identify the region or metropolitan area in which the neighborhood was located, but all specific place-names are fictitious.

WEBSTER TOWNSHIP—SUBURBAN PEACE AND QUIET

Webster Township is contiguous to Illiana, a medium-sized midwestern city and an industrial and educational center. In 1960 the population of the township was 15,000, of whom 45 were classified by the U.S. Bureau of the Census as nonwhite. By our definition, Webster Township is an open neighborhood.

The township occupies an area of slightly more than 17 square miles and in both population density and land use is in no way unusual for an area adjacent to an urban center. The southern quarter of the township is distinctly suburban with new homes in developments and on large wooded lots. To the north, land use becomes less dense and edges on the semirural.

Census data reveal little that is special about Webster Township except for the high proportion of homeowners, the majority of whose homes are in excellent condition. The area's fairly rapid growth is indicated by the fact that as of 1960 slightly fewer than one-third of the houses had been built in 1939 or before. One-fourth of the children attended non-public (presumably Catholic) schools, and the average adult had 11 years of education.

A trustee of Webster Township characterized the neighborhood in the following way:

> It's not in the city—it is suburban living with most of the advantages of the city. It's not crowded. People have moved here because a lot of enterprising builders have developed new shiny residential districts. A fairly large part of the community represents the "old settler" complex of a fairly stable community with a long history.

Webster Township's proximity to the city of Illiana and the spaciousness of the lots were often mentioned by our informants as the most important reasons people like living there. As one informant put it, "People feel they are not living too close to anyone else."

The rapid and recent expansion of the urbanized portion of Webster Township is by no means an unmixed blessing. Informants cited a number of problems stemming from the rapid growth of the area. A PTA president observed that the area "lacked a focal point to draw people together." She observed that, although the people lived in Webster Township, their main interests were in the city, so they took no responsibility for local matters. From her point of view there was a lack of communication among residents. Public services have not been provided at a level that the demand warrants, or so many residents feel. The sewers are not up to par, and building and health codes are inadequate and lack uniformity.

Webster Township is evenly split between Protestants and Catholics; ethnic identifications have become so attenuated that none of our informants could identify or even estimate the proportions of the area's various ethnic groups. Few of the neighborhood facilities are racially integrated. Only one Negro family is a member of the local Catholic church, and there was no consensus among community informants whether both white and Negro children attend the public schools. Each time an informant did report that both whites and Negroes attended a particular school, he estimated the proportion of Negro pupils at less than 1 percent of the student body.

One of our four informants reported that only whites were entering Webster Township. Another said that, although both Negroes and whites were currently moving in, he did not remember how the residents reacted to the arrival of the first Negro families. The two informants who did recall the time of desegregation reported that there was no reaction at all on the part of the white residents, and they doubted that the whites were even aware that the township had been integrated. These two informants dated desegregation at 1962. Each reported that whites constituted 99.9 percent of the new residents of the township. The township trustee estimated the total Negro population at from six to eight families. In the view of the informants, the presence of Negro families has never been a public issue.

Inasmuch as our informants' data are sparse regarding the current racial situation in Webster Township and the history of integration there, our understanding would have been limited if these were the only sources of information available. Fortunately the residents' phase of our survey included interviews with five of the Negro families in the township. Probably these families represented more than half of the Negro population of Webster Township.

The five Negro families we interviewed presented a somewhat different picture of Webster Township. These families were strikingly similar in many respects. Three of the men were physicians and two were attorneys. With the exception of one of the attorneys who worked for a poverty program, all earned more than $15,000 a year. None of the wives worked, and each family owned its home.

These families frequently referred to the spaciousness of their lots in Webster Township and the seclusion this afforded. The wife of one of the attorneys explained, "We designed a house and went looking for a wooded area." She reported that they had a four-acre lot, and added, "We know it will be built up around here. We'll just fence ourselves in for seclusion. We both like seclusion, peace and quiet." This same family had a child with a severe physical handicap requiring that he be protected from physical contact with other children.

The wife of the other attorney gave the reason she most liked living there: "The main reason is the quiet. After living in apartments we wanted to be in the suburbs so we wouldn't be talking right into our neighbor's apartment." One of the doctors' wives remarked, "Our closest neighbor is hundreds of feet away. It's quiet." The wife of another doctor said, "It's quiet, I like the openness and the air seems fresher."

In placing a premium on privacy, it is possible that these Negro families were seeking as much invisibility as possible in their new surroundings. Four of the five reported that they were concerned about how Webster Township's white families would treat them. Apart from this specifically racial consideration, however, these families sought many of the same advantages as whites who moved into Webster Township—namely, better housing and freedom from urban noise and crowding.

Of the five Negro families, two reported that there was no reaction from white residents when they moved in. The other three families experienced some hostility when they arrived. The wife of one of the attorneys said:

I understand that one or two tried to circulate a petition to keep us out and that it took pressure on the owner and the real estate company to let us buy here. After they found out we didn't have tails we were accepted. I'm convinced now it was more the owner than the neighbors who rejected us.

One of the doctors' wives who moved into Webster Township in 1965 said that the community reacted emotionally. She reported:

They had several meetings and a lot of talk with the builder. A state civil rights director from the state capital came up [to mediate the situation].

Another doctor's wife described their move in 1962:

We received a few crank phone calls. There was quite a stir shortly after we moved in because another Negro family wanted to move in and I think that was blocked. Perhaps this wouldn't be true now.

Despite the Negroes' apparent search for anonymity in Webster Township, there was some neighboring between them and their white neighbors. For example, a majority of the Negroes reported having "had dinner or a party together at their home or our home" in the past few months with "a white family living in the neighborhood." One of the attorneys' wives was a substitute in a ladies bridge club, but aside from this instance there is no evidence that the social contacts across racial lines were frequent or regular. One wife observed:

It is almost like two worlds here. The women are not at all friendly but the men are. The men stop and talk but the women stay aloof. Some families have moved out because there is this feeling of unfriendliness.

Webster Township represents a class of communities frequently encountered in this study, and one which we feel will become fairly typical in future years. As we shall see, Negro residents of open neighborhoods have uncommonly high status: their median education is sixteen years, and half of them work in the professions. In high status neighborhoods some distance from the Negro ghetto, there is seldom organized group action on the part of white residents to keep the first Negro residents from moving into the community.

The trickle of middle-class Negroes to the suburbs has begun. Although it does not seem likely to accelerate rapidly, it is likely to be a permanent feature of American life, and one that will bring integration—if, initially, only small-scale integration—to a large number of hitherto all-white communities.

RIVER VISTA—STABILITY THROUGH SOCIAL CONTROL

River Vista Housing Cooperative, a complex of six high-rise buildings with approximately 200 apartments in each, is located in an economically and ethnically heterogeneous area of New York City. All six buildings were constructed in 1964; and in this study, they constitute one moderately integrated neighborhood.

After an extended telephone conversation with the principal of the local public elementary school, one of our interviewers noted: "Very few children from River Vista are drawn into P.S. 99. The development is a middle-income co-op set squat in the middle of a poverty area. Most people [in the co-op] send their children to Jewish, Catholic, or private schools." The principal estimated that from 60 to 70 percent of the community surrounding River Vista is Puerto Rican. The PTA president of P.S. 99 estimated that the school is "80 percent Spanish and Negro."

The ethnicity and age of the residents in River Vista are very diverse. Of its 1,200 families, half are Jewish, about 5 percent are Oriental, and from 10 to 15 percent are Negro. Tensions between Jews and non-Jews appear to be heavily overlaid by differences between the generations, with the Jews generally belonging to the older generation. The senior citizens' Golden Age Club was described by a member of the co-op's board of directors as composed entirely of "older Jewish men and women."

The pastor of the Episcopal church serving this section of New York lives in River Vista. When asked to give "the three or four most important problems of the neighborhood," he said:

> There are religious tensions between the Jews and the Christians. There was a menorah and a Christian holly wreath during the recent holidays, and the wreath was torn down. These are cultural problems. [There are] many aged Jewish couples and many young, free couples living together which causes a breakdown. There are quite a few interracial marriages and there is no common ground of communication between them and these older people.

River Vista was integrated from its beginning, and there is no evidence that integration was ever an issue there. Our informants, to a man, either claimed they did not remember how the whites reacted to the community's racial mix, or reported that there was no reaction at all.

The racial composition of River Vista has been stable, and our informants thought it would remain so in future years. Of all residents moving in during the past year, they reported that about 85 percent were white and 15 percent Negro. Further, when asked to estimate what the proportion of Negroes in the development would be in five years, each informant gave a figure very close to his estimate of the present proportion, which is a sign that there will be little change in the current racial balance.

A neighborhood cannot be adequately understood without knowing something about the adjacent communities with which it shares facilities and through which its residents must pass in their day-to-day living. This is especially true for River Vista, where, as noted above, a new middle-class housing development is surrounded by neighborhoods whose residents are poor. We therefore asked our informants to provide information about each of the neighborhoods surrounding River Vista. The average proportion of Negroes in these neighborhoods is slightly over 15 percent, and all of them are ethnically quite heterogeneous, with Puerto Ricans comprising the single largest group. Ukrainians and Jews also lived in the surrounding neighborhoods, as did younger people described by some of the residents as "beatniks." When we asked about tensions between River Vista and its immediate environment, we received the following answers from our informants. The Episcopal clergyman reported:

> Kids from outside the complex come in from the slums and River Vista people want to keep them out.

The member of the co-op's board of trustees said:

> Crime. We have a high crime area on the east. School is a problem for young couples, whether to use public schools, private schools or move out. The surrounding neighborhood is ugly and dirty.

The PTA president observed:

> The children who don't belong in the neighborhood [River Vista] terrorize the mothers and children, I think the people who live in there don't want the surrounding community. They ask you, "Do you live in River Vista?" There's not a real community relationship between River Vista and the surrounding community.

In response to a question about the degree of concern among residents about crime, three of the four informants reported that the people in River Vista were "very worried." None reported that the crime situation had improved in the past few years. Most of the crimes were committed against people—among them, mugging, purse snatching, and attempted rape.

When asked about tensions between River Vista and specific adjacent neighborhoods, the following comments were typical: "They feel others are getting breaks; they resent being poor; and the kids steal." Again: "The old people resent River Vista being middle income instead of low income after the houses were torn down."

The churches and voluntary organizations located in adjacent neighborhoods but also serving River Vista indicate the heterogeneity to be found there: St. Cyril's Ukrainian Church, Upper Metropolitan Protestant Congregation, St. Killian's Roman Catholic Church, Trinity Lutheran Church, Holy Angel Russian Orthodox Cathedral, Emmanuel Synagogue, Hudson Street Settlement House, and one Jewish and one Catholic community center.

A fairly elaborate network of recreational facilities and activities of voluntary groups has evolved within the River Vista housing complex. In addition to the River Vista Golden Age Club, there are three playgrounds on the premises, an indoor "pram room" for preschool children, a River Vista community room, a River Vista Junior League baseball team, and a dancing class for young children. Doubtless, this proliferation of group activity within the community results in part from the fact that the surrounding neighborhoods are considered essentially hostile territory.

River Vista development is a specific example of a more general set of circumstances under which stable integration is possible. When an urban neighborhood is so sharply differentiated from others nearby, it is frequently because a unique combination of resources has been brought together to establish or maintain it. Especially since federal funds for redevelopment have become available, substantial financial and political resources are employed not only to create these new developments but also to maintain and control them, including the racial and social characteristics of their residents. This can be accomplished either directly through imposing quotas or indirectly by constructing housing units only a narrow segment of middle-class society can afford.

Thus, the perceived future stability of River Vista is no illusion. A management firm deals with all prospective occupants, so there is considerably more formal control over racial balance than under normal market conditions. Stability depends on a strong white demand for housing. Although the cost of a River Vista apartment may be somewhat high for Negroes, it is reasonable for many whites, for whom middle-income, conveniently located housing is difficult to find in the New York area. One of our informants mentioned that there is a long waiting list for housing in River Vista, which indicates that the market will remain strong for some time to come.

The major lesson to be learned here, however, is that racial stability frequently depends on a unique convergence of elements outside normal housing patterns. Where institutional, financial, and political forces combine to control the housing market effectively, stable racial occupancy is possible. This phenomenon is seen with increasing frequency in urban renewal and other new middle-class construction—especially in the central city where universities, hospitals, or other large institutions, in cooperation with public agencies, are ready to make extensive investments in rebuilding the surrounding residential areas.

APEX—CROSSROADS IN THE RURAL SOUTHWEST

Census tract 33 is a rural section of Jones County, which is located in the southwestern region of the United States. The tract occupies about 100 square miles in the county's southeast corner and has a population of 5,100 persons, slightly over one-fourth of whom are Negro. The houses are spread fairly evenly across the countryside, with a slight concentration along the county roads that crisscross it. Small communities have formed at the junction of two or more roads. The largest of these is Crockett, with a population of 1,700. Apex, the community we studied, has a population of 800. There are also a number of smaller

crossroads settlements, such as Henry's Corner, Good
Omen, Damascus, and Mt. Nebo. Jackson City, with a population of almost 60,000, is situated in the center of the
county about 20 miles to the northwest of Apex. Economically, the county depends almost entirely on its oil fields
and cattle pastureland, which typify many areas in the
southwestern region of the United States. As one informant put it, "When I grew up here fifty years ago, this area
used to gin between eight and nine thousand bales of
cotton a year. I don't know of any gins now. We went from
a farm community to a cattle-raising community in the
last twenty years."

Because census data are not provided for an area as small
as Apex and its environs, we have applied the data for the
entire census tract to this "neighborhood." According to
the 1960 census, the median educational level in the tract
was slightly over eight years, and the average annual income about $4,000. The mean age of all adults was 51, and
the median age of all residents was 38—overall, these
figures are higher by far than the average of all neighborhoods in this study. The median age of whites was 41,
while that of Negroes was 28. Whereas only one-fourth of
the whole population was Negro, 36 percent of the people
in the area 14-years old or under were Negro.

Two-thirds of the homes in the entire census tract were
owner occupied, and the vacancy rate was lower than the
national average. Slightly more than half the homes were
classified as in sound condition, at least according to the
1960 census. None were in buildings having three or more
separate units. The mean value of owner-occupied homes
was $5,000; the mean monthly rental was $41. Finally, the
average number of persons per household was 3.0—a low
figure compared to other neighborhoods in this study.

The recent history of Apex is aptly summarized by the
president of the Apex Chamber of Commerce:

We have an eighteen-acre industrial site. We sent a wire to
the President of the New York Stock Exchange last year,

offering them the site, tax free for ten years. He answered with a very nice letter and told us we would be considered. We have newspaper clippings from the papers all over the country about this. One said, "Apex would be a city of 800,000 by and by if it got the New York Stock Exchange."

We were an oil town around here and during the oil boom, there were 3,500 people. Then the town was going to nothing—it got down to 500 people back when we started our house drive in about 1956. So we [the Chamber of Commerce] decided to buy up some land tracts and cut them up into city lots and give them away to anyone who would build a home of $5,000 or over. We still have some lots. Twelve of us got together.

I presented a plan to our Rotary group, which doesn't exist now. They were getting ready to disband so they wouldn't do anything with it. So we twelve formed a Chamber of Commerce ourselves. [The informant showed the NORC interviewer an article headlined "The Druggist Who Saved a Dying Town."] We began with twelve lots. People began coming in so fast that our own property owners decided they might as well get some more money for their land. We have paid as much as $400 an acre and turned around and gave it away. I thought it was possible the New York Stock Exchange would seriously consider us. A lot of people laughed, but I knew the publicity might bring others in. That's what a Chamber of Commerce is for —publicity.

Apex's realtor also referred to the lots being given away by the Chamber of Commerce:

We have bought the third subdivision and we will give you a lot 85 x 123 for one dollar if you will build on it. Just gave one away last week. They are very attractive, nice lots too, on good streets, all facilities. We have built about fifty-five modern homes in the last seven years on these give-away lots. That is the way we have kept our town from completely sinking.

Apex's fortunes are looking up. The state is creating a

new lake on its doorstep by damming up local streams. According to one informant, the dam is already completed; the new lake will be connected to an existing lake and between them the two lakes will cover 5,200 acres. Our informants were unanimous in viewing this as a healthy development for Apex's economy. As a potential resort and tourist attraction, Apex will require—and is likely to attract—a wide range of secondary commercial enterprises.

All of our informants reported that the Negroes were scattered throughout the Apex area, although there was a slight concentration just outside of Apex. The racial composition of new residents—that is, those who have moved in during the past year or so—closely approximates the existing racial distribution of about three-fourths white to one-fourth Negro. According to the Apex High School English teacher, who was one of our informants, "The proportions haven't changed greatly in a hundred years."

Both races have been present in the area since it was first settled during the mid-nineteenth century. The first Negroes were apparently employed by the whites, but their economic status appears to have improved, especially during the period of the oil boom when some of them benefited from a general increase in land values.

The rural communities adjacent to Apex are quite similar to it. Each of them centers on a hamlet and the population in each ranges from one-fourth to one-third Negro. In all these areas, this proportion was reported to have remained steady in recent years.

Apex's schools are in the process of desegregation. The industrial school, which has for years been the Negro school, at one time included all twelve grades. The high school grades, however, were integrated into Apex High School so that it now has 152 students, of whom slightly more than half are Negro. While our interviewing was being conducted, the nearby *Jackson City Times* ran a picture of five seniors on the Apex High School football team, which had just won a district championship; four of the five players were Negro. The elementary schools were operating under a freedom-of-choice plan at the time of the interviewing, so that the previously all-white elementary school was 15 percent Negro, whereas the traditionally Negro elementary industrial school remained all Negro. The "colored school" was to be abolished as such, and a district-wide elementary desegregation plan offered in the coming year. None of the informants reported any tensions between groups of students in the school; on the contrary, most of them seemed pleased that the integration of the school had gone so well—an attitude which corresponds to the evaluation of the situation by our interviewing supervisor in Jones County, who reported that "Apex High School has integrated—on the whole, everything progressing nicely in the southeast part of the county."

Apex has, however, a minimum of integration in its recreational facilities and none at all in its churches. A city park is used for picnics and band concerts, and has play equipment for small children. While the majority of our informants reported that the city park was used by both races, our church informant commented: "They can [use it]—it is a city park but I have never seen any Negroes down there." The same lack of consensus about the use of other community recreational facilities suggests that Negro participation, when it exists at all, is minimal.

That there is substantial social segregation in Apex was also suggested by our church informant, a local Assembly of God pastor, when reporting on the activities of the "colored Baptist Church." When asked how active this church was in neighborhood affairs, he explained that in answering he would "have to do a little segregating." He remarked that "in their own affairs, the colored Baptist Church is very strong," then, in explaining the complete segregation of the churches, remarked:

There is no animosity at all between the colored and white church-wise. I have heard them say that they want to go to their own churches. They worship differently and—well, you know, they do differently than we do and would rather go to their own.

Despite the fact that residential racial integration has typified Apex, the community's only real estate man suggested that racial considerations are still relevant. He said that he couldn't sell property to Negroes "in the wrong place" and hope to remain in business. He reported that when "the problem comes up" he simply calls the white neighbor and asks him whether he wants a Negro buying next door. If he doesn't, the realtor tells the Negro prospect that he isn't handling that particular house anymore.

Although our informants were unanimous in predicting that the Negro population of the area would remain at its present level for the foreseeable future, an ex-president of the Chamber of Commerce observed that the percentage of Negroes in the community might even decline in the future. "We don't have many Negroes wanting to come here," he said. "They haven't been given any encouragement to want to come." Another informant remarked: "In our immediate area, so many of our Negroes are going to California and Arizona."

Apex is typical of a large group of substantially integrated neighborhoods, of which the majority of Americans may be only dimly aware. Southern rural crossroads communities seldom make national headlines, yet in such areas whites and Negroes have been living side by side without friction for years and in housing of comparable quality. If one were to apply northern standards to the bare statistical data available, one would conclude that Apex was, or soon would be, a changing neighborhood. Its population is one-fourth Negro, and Negroes comprise a substantial minority of all areas contiguous to the Apex neighborhood.

However, the residential pattern is one of remarkable stability. The racial proportions have remained constant as long as the community leaders can remember, and it is difficult for them to imagine conditions under which racial change would occur. In part, the very low density of the population helps maintain stability. There are no multiunit structures and a good deal of physical space separates the average citizen of Apex from his neighbors. In addition to the geographical separation afforded by low population density, Apex has also experienced marked separation in its institutions as well as in social contacts among its citizens. It is too early to tell whether the recent integration in the schools will make Apex less attractive to whites. Those who would want all-white schools for their children would have to move to Jackson City, where a more northern pattern of residential segregation exists.

Another factor that suggests continued stability in Apex is the absence of a well-defined expansion on the part of the Negro community. Even if the Negro population should increase appreciably, there is plenty of land available to accommodate such an increase, and Negroes would not necessarily compete for white homes under conditions of high housing demand and short supply.

But for now the spirit of Apex was captured by the local high school English teacher who said, "On the social level, I think everyone is pretty much the same. They all have the same interests, likes and dislikes. Everybody supports football, watches T.V., and attends church."

WELLINGTON—THE NEIGHBORS WOULDN'T SPEAK

Wellington, a town about twenty miles from a large New England city, is an open neighborhood with roughly 13,000 people. Twenty-nine of Wellington's citizens were classified as "nonwhite" in the 1960 census. Of our four neighborhood informants, one, a past president of the Jaycees, reported that only white families were currently moving into Wellington. Another informant, the owner of a real estate firm who had been active in the town for the past fifteen years, reported that both whites and Negroes were currently moving into Wellington, but he did not remember how the community reacted when the first Negro family moved in. The fact that only two of the four community leaders knew that Negroes were moving in and could report on the community reaction suggests that race was not a salient community issue.

Census data for 1960 reveal nothing exceptional about Wellington. One-third of its residents were of foreign stock; the average adult had ten and a half years of education; almost half the residents had lived in a different dwelling five years before; mean income was $7,300; and the mean housing value of homes was $13,000.

Wellington's population is relatively young. The mean age of the adults in 1960 was 43, and the median age of all residents was 24.5—a figure that is lower than all but a handful of the neighborhoods included in this study. A high proportion of the residents own their homes, which are in general of modest size.

According to our informants' estimates, Protestants and Catholics each comprise slightly less than half of Wellington's total population, while Jews account for between 5 and 10 percent of the population. Ethnically, the neighborhood is quite heterogeneous; the largest single group are the Irish, but they account for only roughly 30 percent of the town's population. Although Catholics are well represented in Wellington, neither of the two large parishes maintains a parochial school; less than 2 percent of the children attend non-public schools. Wellington is proud of its local schools, which one informant described as "right up there with the best of them."

Our informants viewed Wellington as offering the major benefits of both urban and suburban living. Its residents are spared living inside the large nearby city, although many of them work and shop there. They feel they can enjoy the advantages of suburban living without paying the high housing costs typical of suburbs closer to the city. The realtor among our informants observed that a home which sold for $20,000 in Wellington would be 20 percent higher in a town closer to the center of the metropolitan area. "You get a much better value when you move out further." On the debit side, Wellington lacks recreational facilities and, according to a majority of the informants, the center of town is unappealing in appearance.

Wellington is a very active community. Our informants identified thirteen different "important neighborhood organizations"—among them, the Junior Chamber of Commerce, Rotary, Lions Club, VFW and American Legion, and a "civic club." There is also a full range of children's organizations, including a number of Boy Scout and Cub Scout troups, Girl Scout and Brownie troups, Campfire Girl groups, and a large number of church-related youth organizations.

Most of the community facilities are racially integrated, at least on a token basis. Many of the main-line churches contain both whites and Negroes, but in each case our informants reported that Negroes accounted for less than one-half of 1 percent of the total church membership. Indeed, the pastor of the largest Roman Catholic church gave "one-fiftieth of 1 percent" as the Negro percentage in his congregation. Similarly, according to the superintendent of schools, each of the nine public schools was integrated, but in each case integration meant one or two Negro students in a school.

Wellington is surrounded by towns that are also virtually all white. All estimates of the Negro proportion in adjoining communities were 1 percent or less. The average estimate of the distance to the "nearest predominantly Negro area" was sixteen miles. When asked what they felt the Negro proportion of Wellington might be in five years, all but one of our informants estimated one-half of 1 percent or less; the school superintendent felt that the proportion might rise as high as 5 percent.

The two informants who recalled Wellington's initial reaction to Negroes moving in painted opposing pictures of the community's response to integration. When asked "What was the community's reaction?" the school superintendent said, "Favorable, that's all I can say." On the other hand, the assistant pastor of the major Roman Catholic congregation said:

Poor. The people were given a hard time. There was a lot
of talk and no friendliness was shown to them. There was a
petition passed around to keep the Negroes out but they
moved in just the same.

The pastor would not go so far as to characterize the
community's response as one of "panic," nor did he report
that there were any organizations which made concerted
efforts to keep Negroes out. There was no violence accompanying the Negroes' arrival, nor did real estate brokers
encourage white families to move out. The pastor was the
only informant to identify two groups that "generally
favored the first Negro families moving into the community"—the Wellington Human Rights Commission
and the Social Action Committee of the Methodist church.
He explained:

I hope and I think we may have a few more Negro families. We haven't had much luck in recruiting them. The
people on the Human Rights Commission feel the town is
being discriminated against by the Negroes. Those
Negroes who can afford to move out of the ghetto prefer to
move to a more affluent community, or they may want to
look at a place where they are closer to their work.

The Clays are the family that integrated Wellington.
John Clay and his wife Dorothy live in a four-bedroom
home with their five children and Mrs. Clay's mother. Mr.
Clay is a consulting engineer in electronics and chemistry
and works out of his home. Both he and his wife have
Ph.D.'s, Mr. Clay in engineering and his wife in biochemistry.
Mr. Clay's report of the reception he received when his
family integrated Wellington corresponds quite closely to
the report given by our church informant, who was assistant pastor at the Catholic church the Clays attend. At a
number of points during the interview, Mr. Clay said that
he bought this home because of the opposition he encountered from the white residents at the time he was considering the move, which occurred in 1955.

I bought it because of the opposition. The minute I looked at the house, there was a petition circulated to keep me out. At that time only 7,000 people lived in Wellington, but there were 10,000 signatures on the petition.

He explained that the realtors in town threatened the bank at which he applied for his mortgage by saying they wouldn't send any more business in the bank's direction if the mortgage were granted; they also threatened to take their savings out of the bank.

Recalling his own experience when he first moved into Wellington, Mr. Clay reported:

They pestered over the telephone in vulgar language. They wanted the stores not to sell me food. Little children asked their mothers at church, "Are those the Niggers you told us about?" That was enough.

Some neighbors wouldn't speak at all, while others would speak here in the neighborhood. But when we would meet them any place else, they would be busy looking the other way.

The Clay family has brought token integration to a substantial range of community facilities. Bobby is the only Negro boy at Fernwood Elementary School, and the Clay family comprises the entire Negro population of St. Agatha's Church. (When asked what proportion of the members of his church were Negro, Mr. Clay said, "Just the eight of us.") Bobby is a Boy Scout, and practices with the Little League baseball team several times each week. (Mr. Clay reported that Bobby "was the most valuable player last year.") When asked if he had any plans to move from Wellington in the next few years, Mr. Clay answered: "No, I will stay here and make the people like it."

There is virtually no Negro demand for housing in Wellington. It is a substantial distance from any concentration of Negro families, and the areas surrounding it are all white. It is unlikely that Negroes will move into Wellington in substantial numbers in the near future because of its distance from the center of the metropolitan area. It is quite possible, however, that a small number of Negro families will move to Wellington since its housing is priced at a level they can afford, and because they may be attracted by the new electronics and other light industrial firms that have been set up there.

> I call the majority of people in there low white trash. The houses were cheaply built to begin with and put up in a hurry, and now most of them are very run down. It's a mess.

The speaker owns a real estate firm in a small town about an hour's drive from downtown Manhattan. She was referring to another of the open neighborhoods in this study, Manor Homes, which was developed during the postwar building boom of the late 1940's. Manor Homes has roughly 500 homes and comprises about half the town of Hemlock.

The 1960 census showed the population of Manor Homes to be less than 1 percent nonwhite, quite average by most measures of socio-economic status, and its residents appeared to be slightly younger and more mobile than the people in most American neighborhoods.

Two-thirds of Manor Homes' residents are Catholic, though their ethnic origins are quite heterogeneous. Each of our informants reported that the population was divided equally among the Irish, Germans, Polish, and Italians. The estimate of the number of Negro families living in Manor Homes ranged from six to eight.

The communities surrounding Manor Homes are practically all white. The town north of Hemlock, all informants agreed, is completely white, while the town to its south is, at most, 2 percent Negro. That part of Hemlock outside of the Manor Homes development does contain a scattering of Negro families—about one in every twenty. The nearest predominantly Negro area is at least ten miles

away. Thus a substantial influx of new Negro residents
into Manor Homes or into the town of Hemlock seems
very unlikely.

The first Negro families moved into Manor Homes in
1964. Each of our informants was present at the time, and
each reported that there was no reaction on the part of the
neighborhood's white residents. As the pastor of the
Catholic church put it: "There was no community reaction. In fact we sort of expected some comment but there
was absolutely nothing." The vice-president of the local
bank, who was also an officer in the Chamber of Commerce, recalled:

> There was no reaction at all. The Negroes that live there
> are children of families that have been in town for many
> years in a different area. I think a couple of whites may
> have put their homes up for sale but there was no other re-
> action.

The eight Negro families in Manor Homes were
reported to be scattered throughout the development and,
according to the realtor, were fixing up their houses. She
added: "If you want to know, they are the nicest people."

The level of integration in community institutions
reflects the token presence of Negroes in the town of
Hemlock. A few Negro students attend the elementary and
the high school. In the children's groups, Negroes participate only in the Boy Scouts, not in the 4-H club or the
youth organizations of the Catholic Church. All the community organizations—the American Legion, the Catholic
parish societies, and the women's club—are exclusively
white. The Lions Club, however, does have Negro
members.

Our informants were hard put to comment favorably on
life in the Manor Homes development. They frequently
used the phrase "in there" when referring to the neighborhood, implying that it was set apart from the rest of the
community and had rather unique characteristics. We
asked our informants to give "the three or four most im-

portant reasons people like living in the neighborhood."
Their responses to this open-ended question are instructive. The pastor of the Catholic parish commented:

> The first reason would be to get away from congested city
> areas. The price of the house is reasonable to people who
> are not able to afford better housing. Other than the fact
> that they can live in a suburban atmosphere for a reason-
> able price, I'm at a loss to pinpoint any reason they like to
> live there.

In answer to the same question, our other informants
were somewhat less charitable although their responses
were similar to that of the Catholic pastor. The bank vice-
president answered:

> The only thing I can think of is that the types of home are
> reasonable but small. Other than that I haven't the slight-
> est idea why anyone should want to live there. I think it's
> like a jungle.

The real estate owner said:

> Because it's a low-income group. They can get reasonable
> housing in that section that they buy on GI or FHA
> financing with no down payment. It's convenient to every-
> thing. I can't think of any other reason—I wouldn't live
> there at all.

When describing the "three or four most important
problems of the neighborhood," the Catholic priest said:

> There is quite a turnover in there. A turnover of people
> and houses. The families are large and they outgrow this
> very small type of housing. What I would say is the single
> most important problem would be financial. They are in a
> sort of general category of low middle income—it's a
> struggle for a number of them. From this single factor
> come all the other things—lack of education, low standard
> of living, apathy and family bickering.

The banker included among the three or four most important problems of Manor Homes:

There are too many children for such a small amount of area. You take your life in your hands if you drive your car down one of those streets. The whole section was put up over night and the streets were made much too narrow. I guess the real problem is the people themselves. Most of them came in from the big cities—I think 50 percent are from city slums and they have no pride of ownership about their property or any pride among themselves. There's a lot of drinking and fighting that goes on in there. When you get this kind of people into a small congested housing area you're bound to have problems.

Yet Manor Homes is a neighborhood where desegregation has proceeded rather smoothly, and race is less of an issue than might have been predicted, given the characteristics of its white residents. Most of these appear to be living on the economic margin, with a substantial part of their incomes going toward payments on their $16,000 homes. In our informants' view, many of the white residents of Manor Homes are emigrants from the industrial central cities of the New York metropolitan region.

Socially and economically, Manor Homes' population is similar to that found on the fringe of expanding Negro ghettoes in many cities; indeed it is from precisely this stratum of white society that the bitterest opposition to integration is normally heard. Manor Homes, however, is different in that it is far removed from any area where there is a heavy concentration of Negroes. This being the case, there is low Negro demand for housing. The prospect of a substantial Negro influx is very remote; our informants' projections on the likely percentage of Negroes in Manor Homes five years hence ranged from 2 to 10 percent.

Thus Manor Homes exemplifies the crucial role played by the degree of Negro demand—sometimes called "Negro pressure"—on a neighborhood. The same group of residents, if faced with the probability of a large influx of Negroes, undoubtedly would have reacted with more hostility to the prospect of integration. Indeed, other neighborhoods included in this study where the socio-economic status of the white residents was higher than Manor Homes, but which were on the verge of a substantial Negro influx, frequently experienced panic and anti-Negro violence.

MILLER HILL—FACING THE BULLDOZER

Miller Hill is a neighborhood occupying a little more than a square mile near the center of a medium-sized city on the eastern seaboard. The city itself lies within one of the nation's largest metropolitan areas.

The neighborhood, which for the purpose of this study was classified as "open," is virtually all white. Two Negro families have lived there since the 1940's. The head of one of these families held a position of authority in the city's fire department; the other owned a small business. The principal of Central School, the major elementary school serving the neighborhood, reported that no Negro students attended her school. She did say that the second elementary school had a handful of Negro students. Our informants agreed that the neighborhood was half Catholic and half Protestant, though they were generally unable to identify specific ethnic groups. When pressed, two of the informants mentioned the presence of Germans, Italians, Scandinavians, and Irish, but they could not even estimate the proportion that any one of these ethnic groups represented in the neighborhood.

Census data reveal that in 1960 one-fifth of the white residents were of foreign stock; the mean education among all residents 25 and over was 8.4 years, while the mean family income was $6,200. The average home was valued at $7,100; the mean rent was $60. Almost five out of every six housing units were built before 1940.

The overriding fact of life in Miller Hill at the time of our study was that it was a neighborhood faced with urban renewal. The City Council found enough blight in the area to warrant its demolition, and a developer proposed a $150 million redevelopment plan that required clearance of the entire neighborhood. Neighborhood residents had formed a committee to take their opposition to the redevelopment plan into the courts. At issue was the designation of Miller Hill as a blighted area, which the residents disputed but which had been upheld in the State Superior Court. According to the local press, a state judge "said 53 percent of the dwellings were substandard in the area the group maintained was not blighted. He added that other blight conditions also were present."

To the west of Miller Hill is an area whose population was estimated by our informants as 80 percent Negro. Moreover, the Negro population in this neighborhood has increased substantially in recent years. Yet the people of this adjoining neighborhood do not share schools or recreational facilities with Miller Hill, nor do the residents of the two communities socialize. The two neighborhoods do not actually have a common border but are separated by a river and some adjacent land, which affect the relationships between them, according to the pastor who was our church informant in Miller Hill. "The city dump and the river are in between," he said, "but if we really bordered them, I think we'd have more problems."

At the southern tip of Miller Hill is Abbott Homes, a public housing project commonly viewed as a problem. Indeed, one of the informants explicitly excluded Abbott Homes from the boundaries of the community. The informants all shared a common attitude toward this housing project, a point of view best summarized by a real estate man:

> First, the village was federal housing, then during Roosevelt's last administration it was transferred to the city. So it is low-rent housing, and these children come to Lincoln School, and some people around here prefer Central School because of that element from Abbott Homes.

> Every tenant I've ever rented to that came from the homes has proved to be a bad tenant.

What is happening now is that colored are demanding to
live in Abbott Homes, so now they are putting Puerto
Ricans and colored in there, and of course that is affecting
Lincoln School. These are not especially poor people; some
can afford to pay a good rent, but they are undesirable people. The city charges them for what they can pay.

The handful of new Negro residents in Miller Hill has
not received a cordial reception. Paint was thrown on the
house of one Negro family who had moved in the summer
before our survey; in another instance, paint was thrown
on an automobile. Our church informant, the local Episcopal pastor, reported:

The clergy went down and cleaned up the fellow's house.
We took up money and had the other man's car repainted.
I think all the clergy took part.

Our real estate informant said:

The Lutheran minister got the other ministers to clean it
up. They even cleaned the inside of the house and she [the
housewife] stood and watched. Most people have to clean
their own houses when they move in.

The role of the above-mentioned Lutheran clergyman in
the desegregation of Miller Hill is unclear. One of our informants claimed that it was he who "got them to move
in." But then he added, "He's [the clergyman] not here
anymore because of all this."

These acts of vandalism against the property of the first
Negro family were an outcropping of general neighborhood hostility against desegregation. The mildest refer-
ence to the community response was from our school informant, who reported "a little fuss." On the other hand, one
informant, a man active in the Boy Scouts, used the term
"community combustion" to characterize the response of
the neighborhood at the time of integration. He reported
that the arrival of the first Negro family "caused great feelings of fear and unrest for a very brief time."

In sum, Miller Hill is a neighborhood with a range of

problems that derive from the age and condition of its housing and the racial composition of the neighborhood to its west. Surrounded by railroad tracks, a city dump, and a polluted river, the older residents look with little enthusiasm to the neighborhood's future. The Boy Scout leader observed:

> The moral fiber goes down as the influx of welfare recipients comes in. An apathetic feeling has come over the neighborhood due to the lowered economic standing of the newcomers.

The Episcopal pastor felt much the same, though he phrased it differently:

> When a neighborhood is on the skids, well, the new people are not about to stay very long. This new group probably moved to get out of areas that are becoming more Negro, and they can't afford to go out to Cedar Heights or the nicer areas. This neighborhood is all they can afford.

Miller Hill, then, is a community that has more than its share of the problems confronting many communities in urban America. Racial integration is but one of a full set of problems that a neighborhood "on the skids" encounters.

SUMMARY

These, then, are six of the 200 integrated neighborhoods whose characteristics are summarized in the balance of this book. The reader, in studying the various tables and statistics, should remember that the neighborhoods described in this chapter are a cross section of the entire sample. Most are overwhelmingly white, and at some distance from the ghetto. Comparatively few are located in the central cities of the urban North.

Finally, this chapter emphasizes the individuality of the neighborhoods and their environments in the face of the necessary summarization that ensues.

3

The Extent of Racially Integrated Housing in the United States

I think in any neighborhood they wouldn't like it [if Negro families tried to move into this neighborhood]. The first reaction is we don't want them here. It would be true of all white neighborhoods. I speak from experience. I saw what happened where I lived.

School principal in white
segregated neighborhood

THERE IS widespread belief among Americans, regardless of their own attitudes toward racial integration, that stable racially integrated neighborhoods are a rare phenomenon. The mass media contribute to the perpetuation of such beliefs in their reporting on "pioneering" integrated neighborhoods and on the problems facing changing neighborhoods. For example, the *New York Times,* in a series of articles surveying housing integration in the nation, quoted a "knowledgeable authority" in St. Louis as saying: "There isn't a white neighborhood anywhere in St. Louis that you could have a colored family move in without it falling apart at the seams [Rugaber, 1966]." Even staunch supporters of integrated living who currently live in integrated neighborhoods believe that theirs is one of the few such neighborhoods in the country.

Our study has uncovered information that contradicts these beliefs. We find that integrated neighborhoods are much more common than most Americans think. We estimate that 36 million Americans in 11 million households live in integrated neighborhoods. This is 19 percent of the

U.S. population, or almost one person in five. The number of households in integrated neighborhoods, although a minority, stands about halfway between the 14 million Roman Catholic households and the 7 million Baptist households in the entire United States; or, to use a more frivolous analogy, it is just about the same number of households that have a home freezer or two or more cars.

ESTIMATES OF HOUSING INTEGRATION

Table 3.1 gives the estimated number of integrated neighborhoods and households in the United States as of April 1967. Among integrated neighborhoods, there are more households in open neighborhoods and neighborhoods in localities with few Negroes than in the three remaining types of integrated neighborhoods.

While the number of substantially integrated neighborhoods (1,830) is relatively large, the small number of households *per neighborhood* yields a national total of only 1.8 million households. Conversely, although the number of open neighborhoods is smaller (1,494), open neighborhoods have about twice as many households per neighborhood as substantially integrated ones, with moderately integrated neighborhoods falling somewhere in between the other two. The average open neighborhood contains 2,160 households; the average moderately integrated neighborhood has 1,640 households; and substantially integrated neighborhoods average 980 households. The integrated neighborhoods in localities with very few Negroes approximate the open neighborhoods in averaging 1,940 households each; the rural areas have only 420 households in an average neighborhood.

Region, size of place, and urbanization account to some degree for the varying number of households in the different types of integrated neighborhoods. In the South, where, for historical reasons, most of the residents of integrated neighborhoods live in substantially integrated

Table 3.1 *Estimated Number of Integrated Neighborhoods and Households in the United States, April 1967*

Neighborhood Type	Estimated Number of:		Percent of Total Households
	Neighborhoods	Households	
Total integrated	8,716	11,198,400	19.0
Open	1,494	3,225,200	5.5
Moderately integrated	1,493	2,451,200	4.2
Substantially integrated	1,830	1,788,000	3.0
Integrated in localities with very few Negroes	1,376	2,670,000	4.5
Integrated rural areas	2,523	1,064,000	1.8
Total segregated	36,884	47,601,600	81.0
Total	45,600	58,800,000	100.0

neighborhoods, the neighborhoods are more likely to be rural and so have smaller populations. In the other regions, suburban and nonmetropolitan neighborhoods that have fewer substantially integrated neighborhoods also tend to be smaller.

Even after controlling for region, size of place, and urbanization, the population of substantially integrated neighborhoods is still less than it is in open neighborhoods. Two explanations are possible:

1. Some substantially integrated neighborhoods cover smaller areas than open neighborhoods. These neighborhoods may have been developed by a single builder, whereas the open neighborhoods were built by several developers over a longer time. For other substantially integrated neighborhoods, which are bordered by all-Negro or changing neighborhoods, neighborhood boundaries may be redefined to exclude portions of the area that earlier had been considered as part of the neighborhood.

2. Some substantially integrated neighborhoods are less densely populated than open neighborhoods. The racial composition of the area may not be important to the residents if the houses are far apart. Also the density of an area is related to the proportion of rental units, so that it may be that white homeowners are more willing to live in (or less able to move out of) substantially integrated neighborhoods than renters.

The density issue is not critical and is only raised here because we suspect that many readers would wonder, as we did, why there are more substantially integrated neighborhoods but more households in open neighborhoods.

REGIONAL VARIATION IN INTEGRATION

Integrated neighborhoods are found everywhere, but the highest percentage of households in integrated neighborhoods, 32 percent, is in the Northeast (Table 3.2). The West, with 26 percent of households, is the next most highly integrated. The South is least integrated, although

Table 3.2 Estimated Number of Integrated Neighborhoods and Households by Region,[a] April 1967

Region and Neighborhood Type	Estimated Number of:			Percent of Total Households
	Neighborhoods		Households	
Northeast:				
Total integrated	2,480		4,592,440	31.8
Open		1,158	2,272,800	15.7
Moderately integrated		773	1,543,360	10.7
Substantially integrated		357	419,280	2.9
Integrated in localities with very few Negroes		192	357,000	2.5
Total segregated	8,270		9,854,560	68.2
Total	11,200		14,447,000	100.0
North Central:				
Total integrated	1,271		2,064,360	12.6
Open		124	462,400	2.8
Moderately integrated		208	319,040	2.0
Substantially integrated		372	427,920	2.6
Integrated in localities with very few Negroes		567	855,000	5.2
Total segregated	11,429		14,346,640	87.4
Total	12,700		16,411,000	100.0

South:			
Total integrated	3,765	2,050,720	11.3
Open	42	120,000	0.7
Moderately integrated	220	141,600	0.8
Substantially integrated	980	725,120	4.0
Integrated rural areas	2,523	1,064,000	5.8
Total segregated	10,435	16,183,280	88.7
Total	14,200	18,234,000	100.0
West:			
Total integrated	1,200	2,490,880	25.6
Open	170	370,000	3.8
Moderately integrated	292	447,200	4.6
Substantially integrated	121	215,680	2.2
Integrated in localities with very few Negroes	617	1,458,000	15.0
Total segregated	6,300	7,217,120	74.4
Total	7,500	9,708,000	100.0

[a] The regions are defined as follows, using the standard census definitions:

Northeast—Maine, New Hampshire, Vermont, Massachusetts, Rhode Island, Connecticut, New York, New Jersey, and Pennsylvania;

North Central—Ohio, Indiana, Illinois, Michigan, Wisconsin, Minnesota, Iowa, Missouri, North Dakota, South Dakota, Nebraska, and Kansas;

South—Delaware, Maryland, District of Columbia, Virginia, West Virginia, North Carolina, South Carolina, Georgia, Florida, Kentucky, Tennessee, Alabama, Mississippi, Arkansas, Louisiana, Oklahoma, and Texas;

West—Montana, Idaho, Wyoming, Colorado, New Mexico, Arizona, Utah, Nevada, Washington, Oregon, California, Alaska, and Hawaii.

the difference between 13 percent in the North Central region and 11 percent in the South is small. Of the 4.6 million households in integrated neighborhoods in the Northeast, about half are in open neighborhoods. Only .4 million are in substantially integrated neighborhoods; the rest are located in moderately integrated neighborhoods. Almost one-third of all these households in integrated neighborhoods are in the New York metropolitan area. To oversimplify, then, the Northeast may be characterized as a region where there are many integrated neighborhoods, but where the proportion of Negroes in any one neighborhood is typically small.[1]

A slightly different picture is observed in the West, where about 60 percent of the households in integrated neighborhoods are in localities with few Negroes (for example, Phoenix, Arizona, or San Jose, California). The remaining 40 percent are pretty evenly distributed among the other types of integrated neighborhoods.

The North Central states are much like the West except that the overall level of integration is lower. Slightly less than half of the households in integrated neighborhoods are in localities with very few Negroes. The rest are split among the other types of neighborhoods.

As might be expected, the southern pattern is substantially different from that in other regions. There is a bitter joke told by Negroes about whites that illustrates this difference. "In the South, they don't care how close you get as long as you don't get too big. In the North, they don't care how big you get as long as you don't get too close." Ap-

[1]In evaluating these estimates, one should keep in mind that they are subject to sampling errors. While the relative error is only about 10 percent on the estimate of the total households in integrated neighborhoods in the United States (1,184,000/11,198,400), relative sampling errors for regions are about two and one-half times as large as sampling errors for the United States, and sampling errors for type of integrated neighborhood within region are five times as large. The data are presented by detail in the tables so that all the numbers will add to the total number of households, but small differences should not be taken too seriously. Most of our discussion is based on differences that are far larger than would be expected due simply to sampling variability.

proximately half of the households in integrated neighborhoods are in rural areas that, according to our informants, have traditionally been integrated. Many of these areas, although not all, are quite poor; and it is mainly in the South that poorer whites and Negroes live together. The remaining households are primarily in substantially integrated areas that have also been integrated for a long time.

There are very few open or moderately integrated neighborhoods in the South. While we do not have past survey data, our study, coupled with the Taeubers' (1965) studies of the South, suggests that in the cities, particularly in the Deep South, whites and Negroes are more segregated today than at the turn of the century. Our definition of integration excluded those areas where whites lived in substantially better housing than Negroes, a common practice in the past. Nevertheless, we do not find poor whites and Negroes living together in the cities, as they did when there were more rigid social class distinctions. Today, segregated housing in the South separates the races and serves the same function as the caste system did earlier.

What little integration there is in the South is mainly in the Southwest and in the border states. Our sample contains no urban integrated neighborhoods in the Deep South and relatively few rural areas. Migration trends indicate that the number of households in integrated rural neighborhoods has declined and will continue to decline as rural Negroes move to the North.

URBANIZATION

Almost a third of all of the households in integrated neighborhoods are in suburbs of metropolitan areas. Although suburbs still have a smaller proportion of Negroes than central cities, the fact that most households in integrated neighborhoods are in open neighborhoods suggests that future increases in integration, if they occur, will be more likely to occur in the suburbs. Of the 3.3 million households in the suburbs, almost half are in open neighborhoods, and only .5 million are in substantially integrated neighborhoods.

In the central cities of metropolitan areas, households are fairly evenly divided among open, moderately integrated, and substantially integrated neighborhoods. This fact, coupled with the greater demand for Negro housing in central cities, suggests that substantially more Negroes could move into the suburbs without affecting the stability of integrated neighborhoods. The growth of suburban populations relative to those of central cities and nonmetropolitan areas would mean an increase in the number of households in integrated neighborhoods in the suburbs, even if the proportion of Negroes in integrated neighborhoods does not change.

Outside of metropolitan areas, integrated neighborhoods are mainly in localities with very few Negroes, or in southern rural areas. The rural areas are not likely to become any more integrated since there is no trend toward Negro or white migration into them. Today integration is a metropolitan phenomenon and it will probably become more so in the future.

THE NUMBER OF NEGRO HOUSEHOLDS IN
INTEGRATED NEIGHBORHOODS

It may seem paradoxical, but a smaller proportion of Negroes than whites live in integrated neighborhoods. Most whites who live in integrated neighborhoods live in open or moderately integrated neighborhoods, or in localities with few Negroes. The percentage of Negroes in these neighborhoods is less than the total percentage (10.5) of Negroes in the United States. Most Negroes who live in integrated neighborhoods live in substantially integrated neighborhoods. Eighty percent of the whites who live in integrated neighborhoods live in neighborhoods with fewer than 10 percent Negroes, while two-thirds of the

Negroes who live in integrated neighborhoods live in neighborhoods with more than 10 percent Negroes. There is every reason to believe that this difference will affect attitudes and behavior, particularly social relationships between the two races.

The regional breakdown shown in Table 3.3 indicates that a higher proportion of Negro households are in integrated neighborhoods in the West than in the other regions. Almost a quarter of western Negroes live in integrated neighborhoods, while in the Northeast and North Central regions, one-sixth of all Negro households are in integrated neighborhoods. In the South, about 10 percent of the Negro households are in integrated neighborhoods. Although the percentage is lowest, the total number of Negroes living in integrated neighborhoods is highest in the South. About half of this total live in integrated rural areas. Both in the South and West, the proportion of Negro households in integrated neighborhoods is about the same as the proportion of white households. In the North Central states, the proportion of Negroes living in integrated neighborhoods is higher than the proportion of whites, but the reverse is true in the Northeast. These differences merely reflect the different proportions of open, moderately integrated, and substantially integrated neighborhoods that we discussed above.

PROPORTION OF NEGROES

Since we feel the proportion of Negro households in a neighborhood is especially important for the future of the neighborhood, we reclassified the households in integrated rural areas or in localities with few Negroes in terms of the percentage of Negro households in the neighborhoods, and we further subdivided households in moderately and substantially integrated neighborhoods. The resulting data suggest no new conclusions, but they indicate quite clearly that the median proportion of Negro households in in-

Table 3.3 Estimated Number and Percentage of White and Negro Households in Integrated Neighborhoods in the United States and by Region, April 1967

Region and Neighborhood Type	White Households		Negro Households	
	Estimated Number	Percent	Estimated Number	Percent
United States:				
Total integrated	10,438,200	19.6	760,200	13.6
Open	3,222,000	6.1	3,200	0.1
Moderately integrated	2,402,800	4.5	48,400	0.9
Substantially integrated	1,291,400	2.4	496,600	8.9
Integrated in localities with very few Negroes	2,606,000	4.9	64,000	1.1
Integrated rural areas	916,000	1.7	148,000	2.6
Total segregated	42,761,800	80.4	4,839,800	86.4
Total	53,200,000	100.0	5,600,000	100.0

Northeast:				
Total integrated	4,432,400	32.8	160,040	17.0
Open	2,270,600	16.8	2,200	0.2
Moderately integrated	1,511,200	11.2	32,160	3.4
Substantially integrated	297,600	2.2	121,680	13.0
Integrated in localities with very few Negroes	353,000	2.6	4,000	0.4
Total segregated	9,075,600	67.2	778,960	83.0
Total	13,508,000	100.0	939,000	100.0
North Central:				
Total integrated	1,875,100	12.3	189,260	16.9
Open	461,900	3.0	500	0.1
Moderately integrated	311,600	2.1	7,440	0.7
Substantially integrated	265,600	1.7	162,320	14.4
Integrated in localities with very few Negroes	836,000	5.5	19,000	1.7
Total segregated	13,412,900	87.7	933,740	83.1
Total	15,288,000	100.0	1,123,000	100.0

(Table 3.3 continued)

Table 3.3 Continued

Region and Neighborhood Type	White Households		Negro Households	
	Estimated Number	Percent	Estimated Number	Percent
South:				
Total integrated	1,748,500	11.5	302,220	9.8
Open	119,900	0.8	100	—a
Moderately integrated	140,000	0.9	1,600	0.1
Substantially integrated	572,600	3.8	152,520	4.9
Integrated rural areas	916,000	6.0	148,000	4.8
Total segregated	13,405,500	88.5	2,777,780	90.2
Total	15,154,000	100.0	3,080,000	100.0
West:				
Total integrated	2,381,200	25.7	109,680	24.4
Open	369,600	4.0	400	0.1
Moderately integrated	440,000	4.7	7,200	1.6
Substantially integrated	155,600	1.7	60,080	13.4
Integrated in localities with very few Negroes	1,416,000	15.3	42,000	9.3
Total segregated	6,877,800	74.3	339,320	75.6
Total	9,259,000	100.0	449,000	100.0

aLess than 0.1 percent.

tegrated neighborhoods is between 1 and 5 percent everywhere except in the South.

This small percentage of Negroes in most integrated neighborhoods may explain why our estimates seem so large compared with popular conceptions. If we think of integrated neighborhoods as only those that are substantially integrated, we would exclude four out of five of our neighborhoods. We believe that the broader definition is a sensible one because it focuses attention on who is moving into neighborhoods rather than on a fixed proportion of Negroes and whites living in neighborhoods. Since the concern for housing integration is primarily a concern for freedom of residence rather than for a particular racial distribution, we believe that neighborhoods which are currently open to both whites and Negroes should be considered integrated.

Currently very few whites are willing to live in neighborhoods where Negroes are in the majority. Of the whites in any kind of integrated neighborhood, slightly less than 1 percent live in neighborhoods that are more than 50 percent Negro. There are, of course, whites who live in neighborhoods with a larger proportion of Negroes, but these are changing neighborhoods and will eventually become all Negro. At present, then, it would appear that the percentage of Negroes in the neighborhood is an important variable influencing the housing choice of whites.

SUMMARY

Overall, we find that integrated neighborhoods are much more common than many Americans think they are. As mentioned earlier 19 percent of the U.S. population, or about one person in five, live in integrated neighborhoods. Since this is the first time that national estimates have been made of the extent of integration, we do not know whether the percentage of families in integrated neighborhoods is now higher or lower than it has been, but these estimates provide base-line measures for future studies.

The figure of 19 percent is significant because the neighborhoods represented by this percent of the population are ones into which Negroes have indeed moved, and into which both races are currently moving. This figure becomes more meaningful when it is supplemented by data about the percentage of Negroes in the neighborhoods classified as "integrated." Half of the households in integrated neighborhoods are in neighborhoods where Negroes account for 3 percent or less of the total.

Thus, 81 percent of the nation's households remain in segregated neighborhoods, while roughly 10 percent are in integrated neighborhoods where Negroes represent only 3 percent or less of the neighborhood population. To put it another way, only 4 percent of the households in the United States are located in integrated neighborhoods that are more than 10 percent Negro.

It is probable that a substantial number of white residents in the integrated neighborhoods we studied, because they are in the overwhelming majority, have no social or community-based contact with the few Negroes who live in their neighborhoods. It is even possible that most white residents in some of our integrated neighborhoods are unaware of the presence of any Negroes.

There are substantial regional differences in the proportion of Negroes. The Northeast is the most integrated, a fact due in part to the high level of integration in the New York metropolitan area. Most of the residents of integrated neighborhoods in the Northeast live in open or moderately integrated neighborhoods with relatively few Negro households. In the West, which is the next most integrated region, usually a household in an integrated neighborhood is in a locality with very few (less than 2 percent) Negroes. The same pattern is observed in the North Central region except that the overall level of integration is lower than in the West. In the South, the pattern is quite different, with households in integrated neighborhoods being either in rural areas or in substantially integrated areas that have been integrated for a long time. There are few open or moderately integrated neighborhoods in the South, indicating that integration is probably decreasing in the South.

Most new integration seems to be occurring in the suburbs of metropolitan areas, and, if a small proportion of Negroes is a requisite for stable integration, there are indications that this will be the future trend. At this time, however, central cities are still substantially more integrated than suburbs or nonmetropolitan areas.

Finally, since the median percentage of Negro households in integrated neighborhoods is 3 percent, compared with about 11 percent nationally, the percentage of all Negroes who live in integrated neighborhoods is smaller than the percentage of whites. This is particularly true in the Northeast.

4 The History of Neighborhood Desegregation

A REVIEW OF the history of racial desegregation in the neighborhoods we studied serves two purposes. First, it allows us to examine the prevalent stereotype of the desegregation process that normally includes tension, strife, block-busting, and the exodus of white residents that typically lead quickly to complete racial turnover. Undoubtedly this process occurs under certain conditions and can legitimately be viewed as a social problem. It is possible, however, that the attendant drama and publicity exaggerate its prevalence. Second, knowing about the neighborhoods' histories may provide a better understanding of their present characteristics and the current behavior and attitudes of their residents.

The aspects of the history of integration that concern us in this chapter are the racial composition of a neighborhood at the time it became integrated, the approximate date of desegregation, and the reaction of the neighborhood residents to the entry of the first Negroes. Then, using the reaction of the residents as an independent variable, we analyze the current interracial attitudes and behavior of the residents as well as the current proportion of Negroes in the neighborhood.

For information we relied primarily on the reports of the neighborhood informants, four of whom were usually interviewed in each neighborhood in our sample of integrated neighborhoods and our control sample of segregated neighborhoods. Their responses were combined to obtain a single neighborhood measure for each variable.

The *neighborhood* is the unit of analysis we used, because the informants were responding to questions about one specific neighborhood. However, instead of giving each neighborhood a weight of one, we weighted each by an estimate of the number of residents living there in order to attempt to correct for the fact that the neighborhoods' populations varied widely. This sample weighting procedure was based on the idea that it is the *number of families* characterized by a certain neighborhood factor (say, that the neighborhood was built by a single builder), not the *number of neighborhoods* so characterized, that is crucial.

A second procedure was developed to deal with frequent lack of consensus among the four neighborhood informants. In response to a question about crime in the neighborhood, two of the informants may have said that the residents were "a little worried," but the other two may have replied that the residents were "not at all worried." This problem was resolved by dividing the neighborhood resident weights described above into response categories according to the proportion of informants giving these responses. Or, to use another example, if all the informants reported that a neighborhood originally contained only whites, the entire weight for the neighborhood was allocated to this category. However, if three of the four informants said it was all white and one said it contained both races, 75 percent of the weight was allocated to the former category and 25 percent to the latter. To get the percentages upon which we based our final conclusions, we

totaled the weights within each category and divided these
sums by the total of all of the weights.[1]

All of the neighborhood informants were asked to report
on the history of desegregation in their neighborhoods.
Once a neighborhood was established as integrated, neighborhood informants were asked about the neighborhood's
racial composition "when this neighborhood was first
built." Unless they reported that there were substantial
differences between white and Negro housing, they were
next asked, "In what year did Negroes move into housing
comparable to that of whites?" Table 4.1 shows the data
these two questions yielded from our sample of integrated
neighborhoods and the matched sample of Negro
segregated neighborhoods[2] in the North and West and in
the South.[3]

The most striking finding pertains to regional differences. Of the northern and western integrated neighborhoods in the sample, 84 percent were all white when
first established, and the balance were integrated from the
beginning. In the South, by contrast, only 29 percent of
the integrated neighborhoods were originally established
as all-white communities, while the clear majority, 65 percent, were biracial from the beginning. These figures alone
suggest sharply divergent histories and patterns of change

[1] A computer program was written especially for this procedure by Earl D.
Main, then of the NORC data-processing staff, whose efforts and skill are
gratefully acknowledged.

[2] According to the "process" definition of integration, there may be white residents in a "Negro segregated" neighborhood, since this type of neighborhood is defined by the fact that no whites are currently moving in, not by
any certain racial proportions. Thus, there were instances where whites
comprised a large majority of the residents of a "Negro segregated" neighborhood.

[3] For the most part we have divided the United States into two regions, with
the North and West comprising one and the South the other. Hence,
references to the North (or northern) often include the West (or western).

Table 4.1 *Original Racial Composition of Neighborhood and Length of Time since Desegregation, by Region, for Integrated and Negro Segregated Neighborhoods (Percent of Households: Data from Informants)*

Present Integration Status	Original Racial Composition				Number of Years Since Desegregation[a]
	Contained Only Whites	Contained Only Negroes	Contained Both Races	Total	
	North and West				
Integrated	84	0	16	100	16.8
Negro segregated	66	16	18	100	12.4
	South				
Integrated	29	6	65	100	17.6
Negro segregated	4	18	78	100	9.0

[a] Data not obtained if neighborhood contained only Negroes when first built.

between the two regions. In terms of physical proximity of the races, they suggest change in the North and stability in the South. Similar North-South differences emerge when the Negro segregated neighborhoods are considered. In the North, 66 percent of the neighborhoods now identified as Negro segregated were all white when they were first built, and thus have exhibited complete racial succession. In the South, only 4 percent of the current Negro segregated neighborhoods exhibit a history of complete racial succession.

This information cannot be accurately evaluated, however, without understanding that original racial composition and present status do not necessarily employ the same definition of integration. For a neighborhood to have qualified as currently "integrated," it must have been one where both whites and Negroes were moving into housing of comparable quality at the time of our interviews. This proviso was established because at one time in the South, even though whites and Negroes lived in close physical proximity, the Negro housing was distinctly inferior to that of the whites. The *original* status of a neighborhood, however, was determined on the basis of proximity alone. The data for southern neighborhoods document the fact that, from their inception, Negroes have at least been physically present.

Thus, it is not quite accurate to assume that there has been no change in those neighborhoods in the South that originally "contained both races" and that are at present "integrated." It is likely that in most of these, Negroes have been moving from housing that was comparatively inferior into housing that is now of similar quality to that occupied by white residents.

The second question, how many years has it been since Negroes moved into "housing comparable to that of whites," referred to two different processes, depending on the region in which it was asked. In the North and West the answer undoubtedly identified the year in which Negroes actually first began to move into the neighborhood from elsewhere. In the South, it is likely that the year mentioned marked an upgrading of the housing available to Negroes within the neighborhood rather than the arrival of new Negro residents within its boundaries. This latter seems especially probable given the low population density and semirural nature of many of the southern integrated neighborhoods.

This explains why there is virtually no difference in the length of time since "desegregation" first occurred in northern and southern integrated neighborhoods. It has been almost seventeen years since the first Negroes moved into the northern neighborhoods. In the South, it has been about eighteen years since Negroes moved into housing comparable to that of whites, although in 65 percent of the neighborhoods Negroes have been physically present since the neighborhoods were first established. These figures indicate a longer period of interracial stability than would have been predicted on the basis of popular conceptions.

An important insight into the process of desegregation can be gained by observing that Negroes moved into the Negro segregated neighborhoods more recently than they moved into neighborhoods that are still stable and integrated. As noted above, in the North and West the integrated neighborhoods (into which whites and Negroes are still moving) saw the arrival of the first Negro family about seventeen years ago. Remembering that 3 percent is the median proportion of Negroes in our integrated neighborhoods, it seems safe to predict that most of these neighborhoods will continue to attract white residents and remain integrated, at least in the foreseeable future. In contrast, the Negro segregated neighborhoods in the North and West (into which no whites are moving) experienced their first Negro in-migration only twelve years ago, an indication of rapid change from an all-white status to a changing or mostly Negro status.

Of those northern and western integrated neighborhoods within the central city of a standard metropolitan area (SMSA), only 10 percent were established as communities containing both whites and Negroes. Among those in the suburbs of an SMSA, 21 percent—slightly more than one out of every five—were biracial from the beginning. That more suburban than central-city integrated neighborhoods contained Negroes from the outset may at first seem paradoxical since the majority of Negroes encounter difficulty when they move from central-city areas to the suburbs. The higher suburban percentage can be explained, in part at least, by the fact that most metropolitan areas have had some suburban Negro residents whose origins can be traced back many generations—in some cases to the middle of the nineteenth century when these areas were terminal points for the underground railroad used by southern Negro slaves fleeing to the North before and during the American Civil War.

RESIDENT REACTION TO DESEGREGATION

We also asked the informants to tell us how the white residents reacted to the arrival of the first Negro residents in their neighborhoods. The informants whose responses

we shall discuss here reported on two types of neighborhoods: northern integrated and northern Negro
segregated (*i.e.*, those neighborhoods into which whites are
no longer moving but which still may have white residents). Represented in this group are 108 northern integrated and 17 northern Negro segregated neighborhoods. The reader should recall, however, that the
latter do not constitute a random sample of all northern
Negro segregated neighborhoods. They were selected to be
comparable to the integrated neighborhoods in location
and socio-economic status.

The residents' reactions described by the informants
were classified into the following six categories: positive,
no reaction, mildly negative, overtly negative, hostile, and
violent. Before discussing these reactions, the terminology
we have selected to use should be explained. As we mentioned before, each neighborhood does not have equal
weight; instead, it is weighted in terms of an estimate of
the number of families it contains. That is, more populous
neighborhoods will carry greater weight than those containing fewer residents. Therefore, although it is more
technically correct to say, for example, that "20 percent of
the families living in integrated neighborhoods reacted
positively," we shall use the less cumbersome "20 percent
of the integrated neighborhoods reacted positively."

Turning now to the reactions, Table 4.2 shows that 18
percent of the northern integrated neighborhoods reacted
to the first Negro residents positively. One of our mid-wes-
tern informants in an integrated neighborhood, characterized by well-educated residents and containing relatively few Negroes, said: "They welcomed them with open
arms. No great friction, stress or strain. They are all do-
gooders here."

In 36 percent of the northern integrated neighborhoods
"no reaction" was reported. This response is an accurate
interpretation of the verbatim answers we received; it is,
nevertheless, instructive to note some of the comments
with which the informants amplified their answers. For example:

I haven't heard a comment one way or another. The Negroes were accepted. One is a Ph.D. in chemistry, why shouldn't they be accepted? [Suburban open neighborhood in New Jersey]

They didn't think too much of it, the father was an attorney. [Moderately integrated central-city neighborhood in upstate New York]

No reaction. They were on the same level businesswise and housing-wise, and no one complained. [Moderately integrated suburban neighborhood in Southern California]

Table 4.2 *Community Reaction to Entry of First Negroes and Neighborhood Type (Percent of Households Living in Neighborhoods Which Responded in Various Ways to Arrival of First Negro Family: Data from Informants)*

	Neighborhood Type		
Community Response	*Northern Integrated*	*Northern Negro Segregated*	*Southern Integrated*
Positive reaction	18	14	8
No reaction	36	21	55
Mildly negative: Neighborhood rumors, meetings, petitions, gossip	33	11	0
Overtly negative: Panic, block-busting, white exodus	6	44	15
Hostile: Minor acts of hostility against Negroes	3	13	19
Violent: Major acts of hostility against Negroes	1	20	10

Obviously many informants explained the absence of any reaction on the part of the white community in terms of the social acceptability of the new Negro residents. Where Negroes had occupational and educational characteristics similar to those of the whites, hostility was greatly reduced.

In 43 percent of the northern integrated neighborhoods,

the arrival of the first Negroes evoked some type of negative reaction. In 33 percent of the neighborhoods, the
response was mildly negative, limited to private activity
marked by rumors, gossip, neighborhood meetings, and petitions. Typical of the responses describing this reaction
are the following:

> They hit the ceiling, the people all got up in arms, and
> they were going to sue the builder. Five or six sold their
> homes. A meeting was held and everyone held on.
> [Suburban neighborhood in the Pacific Southwest]

> The whites didn't want them because the majority of the
> houses were owner-occupied. In some cases they convinced
> the Negro to get out. I know two families who owned
> grocery stores and went broke because they rented [houses]
> to Negroes. [Substantially integrated suburban neighbor-
> hood in Texas]

> The next door neighbors didn't like it. They built a big,
> high wooden fence between—not just wire. [Open
> suburban neighborhood in Connecticut]

The remaining reactions that can be classified as overtly
negative, hostile, or violent occurred in a relatively small
percentage of northern integrated neighborhoods. In 6
percent the reaction was classified as overtly negative and
involved panic, block-busting, and attempts by whites to
leave the neighborhood. The following responses are
representative accounts of this type of reaction:

> There was no trouble. The whites began to move out.
> There were signs all over the place. [Substantially in-
> tegrated central-city neighborhood in Michigan]

> There were tensions and I know there were brokers who
> tried to block-bust. I got wind of it and the first time I got
> calls from people to give me listings, I went over and
> talked them out of it. [Open suburban neighborhood in
> New Jersey]

For sale signs sprung up on many lawns. One property sells (to Negroes) and the appraisers lower the value for mortgages. The place becomes a no man's land. The whites won't buy, and as yet the Negroes can't buy, so the actual price is lowered. [Substantially integrated central-city neighborhood in Indiana]

The homeowners' association wasn't positive at that time. They tried to buy houses to keep out the Negroes. I feel if the president at that time had any foresight and positive direction, this would have averted a lot of unrest. [Substantially integrated suburban neighborhood in Michigan]

It was a reaction of panic. Whites had block meetings, and everyone pledged not to sell, and no one kept their word. [Negro segregated central-city neighborhood in Illinois]

In 3 percent of the neighborhoods, the residents reacted with direct action of a hostile nature against the new Negro residents. Typical responses concerning this type of minor act against Negroes are the following:

Anonymous phone calls, only a few signs. Mainly ignoring the Negroes. People just refused to talk to or acknowledge Negroes' presence. [Neighborhood in locality with very few Negroes in Pacific Northwest]

They reacted with maximum resistance just short of violence. Legal maneuvering, neighborhood petitions, threats, phone calls, and other general harassments. [Negro segregated central-city neighborhood in Southern California]

Incidents of window-breaking and tire-slashing by whites. [Negro segregated central-city neighborhood in Illinois]

Finally, in only 1 percent of the northern integrated neighborhoods did the residents respond with actions that could be described as major violence, such as arson or bombing.

Although the experiences of the northern integrated neighborhoods are of interest *per se*, further insight can be gained by comparing them with what happened during the period of desegregation in the northern Negro segregated neighborhoods into which only Negroes are currently moving. The northern neighborhoods that are presently stable and integrated enjoyed a comparatively tranquil period of racial integration compared to the Negro segregated neighborhoods. In 54 percent of the former, there was no negative reaction to the initial arrival of Negroes; whereas in only 35 percent of the latter did the desegregation pass without a negative response. More important, in the northern integrated neighborhoods there was substantially less panic and block-busting (6 percent versus 44 percent), much less hostile action against Negroes (3 percent versus 13 percent), and far fewer acts of violence against Negroes (1 percent versus 20 percent).

All else being equal, the response of white residents to integration is clearly related to the likelihood of the neighborhood's remaining stable—that is, continuing to attract white residents for a number of years. Those white neighborhoods in which the residents are strongly determined to resist Negro integration are eventually likely to change from all white to all Negro. The effort to discourage Negroes from moving in—to "keep them out"—seldom succeeds, but it apparently leaves a legacy of anti-Negro bitterness or fear that encourages a rapid exodus of whites from the neighborhood. The converse undoubtedly also holds true; that is, when attempts are made to welcome the integration of an all-white neighborhood, or where integration passes relatively unnoticed, there is a comparatively good chance that the neighborhood will remain stable and interracial for some time.

Our conclusions thus far are based on responses to a single, open-ended question about the nature of white residents' reactions when the first Negroes moved in. This question was followed by a number of more specific questions that attempted to elicit more detailed information about the negative nature of community reaction (Table 4.3).

Table 4.3 *Negative Reaction to Entry of First Negroes and Neighborhood Type (Percent of Households: Data from Informants)*

| | Neighborhood Type | | |
Community Response	Northern Integrated	Northern Negro Segregated	Southern Integrated
Panic	13	37	4
Violence	2	15	23
Churches were hostile or split	8	33	0
Community organizations were hostile or split	6	22	0
Brokers encouraged whites to leave	12	60	17
Community organizations tried to keep Negroes out	5	22	0

Informants were asked, "Was there any panic in the neighborhood?" Thirteen percent of the integrated neighborhoods and 37 percent of the (now) Negro segregated neighborhoods responded with panic. As Table 4.3 shows, there was consistently a higher percentage of negative reaction in those neighborhoods that have since become Negro segregated than in the integrated neighborhoods.

Although such information is retrospective, and only approximates the kind of continuous study necessary to assess change, the magnitude of these differences and the fact that they were elicited by six different measures of community response indicate beyond a reasonable doubt that a neighborhood's chances for racial stability are severely threatened by anti-Negro sentiments. When such hostility is present, not only is the exodus of whites accelerated when integration occurs, but the neighborhood's attractiveness to new white residents is very greatly reduced.

We also have reports from the residents themselves with which to check the informants' reports about community reaction to racial desegregation. White residents who were living in the neighborhood when the first Negroes moved in were asked a series of questions about their own personal reactions to this event (Table 4.4). In interpreting their replies, especially of those living in Negro segregated (or changing) neighborhoods, it should be remembered

Table 4.4 *Reactions of White Residents to Entry of First Negroes and Present Integration Status of Neighborhood (Percent Giving Selected Responses)*

	Present Neighborhood Integration Status	
Item	Integrated	Negro Segregated
Personal position regarding integration of neighborhood:		
Approved	17	34
Didn't care	63	37
Opposed	20	29
Total	100	100
N	(444)	(42)
Emotional reaction:		
Happy, pleased	7	10
Neutral	77	63
Afraid, worried	16	27
Total	100	100
N	(406)	(30)
Percent who thought of moving	4	9
N	(490)	(44)
General reaction when first Negroes moved in:		
Pleased	5	5
Made no difference	74	53
Unhappy	21	42
Total	100	100
N	(485)	(44)

that we did not question the residents who moved out of the neighborhood after desegregation. In other words, the data in Table 4.4 represent only the reactions of those white residents who have remained in the neighborhood, and not the reactions of *all* of the white residents who lived in the neighborhood at the time desegregation actually began.

The first item in Table 4.4 presents the coding categories established for the residents' open-ended responses to a question about how they felt when the first Negroes moved in. All codable responses were placed into one of five categories ranging from strong approval to strong opposition; the extreme responses have been collapsed to yield three categories: approved, didn't care, and opposed.

In part the data support the conclusion that a hostile response by whites to desegregation is associated with a neighborhood's eventually becoming Negro segregated. The answers from 29 percent of the white respondents in Negro segregated neighborhoods could be classed as clearly expressing opposition; while in the integrated neighborhoods only 20 percent were opposed. However, the percentage reporting approval of desegregation is also higher among those currently living in Negro segregated neighborhoods than among those currently in stable integrated neighborhoods (34 percent versus 17 percent). Since we know that our white residents of Negro segregated neighborhoods are not a cross section of all whites who lived in the neighborhood at the time of desegregation, it is difficult to conclude with confidence what the data would appear to suggest—namely, that Negro segregated neighborhoods are polarized with about one-third of the white respondents favoring and about one-third opposing desegregation.

A more likely explanation is that the composition of the whites in a neighborhood changes as a result of the selective exodus of the white residents when the first Negroes move in. If it is true that those who opposed the desegregation of the neighborhood subsequently moved out, it is probable that the figure of 29 percent opposing integration among those whites who remained is substantially lower than the percentage of all of the white residents who opposed it at the time it occurred in those neighborhoods that subsequently changed.

The same open-ended responses were coded according to their emotional content. Analysis of the first few responses indicated that it was possible for an individual to accept racial integration and still express personal apprehension about its consequences.

As Table 4.4 shows, more residents of Negro segregated neighborhoods than of stable integrated neighborhoods reacted with fear, worry, and tensions (27 percent versus 16 percent); and, although the difference is small, slightly more had a happy or pleased reaction to desegregation of the neighborhood.

When we asked the respondents whether or not they had thought of leaving when the first Negroes moved in, 4 percent of those in integrated neighborhoods and 9 percent in Negro segregated neighborhoods said "yes." The last figure, of course, would have been much higher had we been able to obtain the reaction of those who did move out of the neighborhood prior to our study.

In response to our final and summary question, "In general, were you pleased or unhappy when the first Negroes moved in, or didn't it make any difference?" 42 percent of the white residents in Negro segregated neighborhoods and 21 percent in integrated neighborhoods reported unhappiness.

Thus, the information provided by the residents themselves tends to corroborate our conclusions based on the informants' report of the history of desegregation. Both indicate that neighborhoods which are no longer attracting white residents experienced a more difficult period of desegregation than did those neighborhoods which are currently stably integrated.

There is evidence that the response of the white residents to the arrival of the first Negroes is related to the whites' sense of the probability that "inundation" will occur. One is reminded of Saul Alinsky's testimony at Chicago hearings of the U. S. Commission on Civil Rights (1959) about a white mob that had formed near the home of the first Negro family in a certain neighborhood. He reported walking into the crowd and asking individuals whether they would be this violently opposed to the first Negro family if they could be assured that the proportion of Negroes in the neighborhood would not exceed an agreed-upon level, for instance, 25 percent. The whites consistently responded that they would not be so distressed at the arrival of the first Negro family if the eventual proportion of Negroes could in fact be so controlled, but felt this was obviously impossible. In their minds, the arrival of the first Negro always signaled the beginning of substantial Negro in-migration, and it was this they were fighting.

THE IMPACT OF COMMUNITY RESPONSE

Using information provided by the neighborhood informants, we have tried to measure neighborhood response to desegregation, including the reactions of three types of neighborhood institutions: the churches, the community organizations, and the real estate business (Table 4.3). In addition, we turned to the residents who were present when the first Negro families moved in to learn about their personal reactions to desegregation. We shall now attempt to determine whether the activities of the major neighborhood institutions were associated with the personal reactions of the families residing there.

Table 4.5 presents four different measures of personal response to integration classified by three different measures of institutional activity at the time integration occurred. To explain these data, we shall take as an example the top section of the table. There each resident is classified according to whether a majority of the informants for his neighborhood reported that real estate

Table 4.5 *Personal Reactions of White Residents to Entry of First Negroes and Reaction of Community Institutions, for Integrated Neighborhoods*

Reactions of Community Institutions at Time of Integration	Personal Reactions of White Residents			
	Personal Position (Percent Opposed)	Emotional Reaction (Percent Worried)	Percent Who Thought of Moving	General Reaction (Percent Unhappy)
Real estate brokers encouraged whites to leave:				
Yes	29 (66)[a]	28 (60)	7 (75)	27 (74)
No	19 (288)	14 (261)	2 (319)	20 (318)
Churches favored the integration:				
No	26 (260)	20 (232)	4 (286)	25 (284)
Yes	7 (66)	8 (66)	2 (74)	14 (74)
Community organizations favored integration:				
No	23 (260)	18 (238)	3 (288)	25 (286)
Yes	19 (69)	15 (64)	5 (76)	15 (75)

[a]Figures in parentheses are the number of cases on which the percentages are based.

brokers "had engaged in practices that encouraged white families to move out." Residents of neighborhoods that were so classified were more likely than the residents of other neighborhoods to have opposed the arrival of the first Negro families; to have reported that they were worried or afraid when desegregation began; to have thought of moving at that time; and to have reported that they were "unhappy" when the first Negro families moved in.

Similar patterns emerge when the other two measures of institutional response are employed. Residents are more likely to report negative reactions to desegregation of the neighborhood if it is not characterized as one in which the churches or the community organizations "generally favored the first Negro families moving into" the neighborhood.

The major point of Table 4.5 is reasonably clear: in neighborhoods where the chief institutions fail to respond positively or actually respond in a negative manner, the residents themselves are more likely to oppose the arrival of the first Negroes and to think of moving from the neighborhood.

If it is true that the response of the community at the time desegregation occurs influences the course of later events, this should be most clearly documented in subsequent changes in the proportion of Negroes in the neighborhood. Table 4.5 presented the reactions of the white residents who were present at the time desegregation occurred and who remained in the neighborhood. In choosing to study the present proportion of Negroes in the neighborhood, we are assuming that the rapidity with which whites leave the neighborhood and whether it continues to attract new residents are affected by the events that accompanied the arrival of the first Negroes.

Previously, we compared neighborhoods that were currently integrated (those into which whites continue to move) with Negro segregated neighborhoods (those into which whites no longer move), noting that the latter had responded with greater panic and hostility to desegregation than the former. From this we inferred a cause-effect relationship in which the community's negative response to desegregation was itself a factor precipitating rapid racial change in the neighborhood. In the discussion that follows, we explicitly view the community response as an antecedent, causal factor and treat the current proportion of Negroes in the neighborhood as the dependent variable. The analysis is limited here to the 108 northern and western integrated neighborhoods. All data were provided by neighborhood informants. The mean proportion of Negroes for all these integrated neighborhoods was 6.5 percent.

Table 4.6 employs the six specific "reaction" items first introduced in Table 4.3; the dependent variable is the current percent of Negroes in the neighborhood. For example, where a majority of the neighborhood informants answered "yes" to the question, "Was there any panic in the neighborhood?" Negroes accounted for 10.4 percent of the

Table 4.6 *Percent Negro in Neighborhood, by Community Reaction at Time of Integration, for Northern and Western Integrated Neighborhoods*

Community Reaction	Percent Negro
Panic:	
Yes	10.4
No	5.7
Churches favored the integration:	
Yes	7.1
No	7.7
Community organizations favored the integration:	
Yes	7.7
No	7.3
Real estate brokers encouraged whites to leave:	
Yes	20.6
No	4.1
At least one organization tried to keep Negroes out:	
Yes	11.0
No	6.0

population; in those neighborhoods where a majority of the informants answered "no," the proportion of Negroes was only 5.7 percent.

Consistent with earlier findings, the types of response most strongly associated with subsequent higher proportions of Negroes are the activities of the real estate brokers and the presence of organizations that attempted to keep Negroes out of the neighborhood. The clearest association is with the activity of the real estate brokers. In those neighborhoods where a majority of informants responded "yes" to a direct question about whether real estate brokers encouraged whites to leave, the proportion of Negroes (by the time of this study) had climbed to 20.6 percent; whereas where a majority responded "no," the proportion of Negroes was only 4.1 percent. The reader should recall that this table includes only the integrated neighborhoods. The differences noted in Table 4.6 would undoubtedly have been greater had it also included Negro segregated neighborhoods where the advent of the first Negroes was met with an unusually hostile response.

INTERPRETATION

Although the association between white panic and a rapid rise in the level of Negro occupancy seems clear enough, interpretation of changing neighborhoods can be somewhat more complex. The first and simplest way of looking at the data is to assert, as has been done at various points in this chapter, that opposition to the arrival of the first Negroes breeds fear and anti-Negro feelings that then become the basis for a more rapid emigration of white residents from the neighborhood. This is a simple cause-and-effect point of view, where white hostility is the "independent variable" that leads to a greater white exodus.

But a second perspective is also possible. Both white hostility at the time of desegregation and subsequent departure from the neighborhood can be viewed as but two facets of the same general mode of response to other factors which existed previously. Such a factor might be the degree of Negro demand for housing in the neighborhood, which has two separate effects: a hostile response to desegregation and more rapid white emigration from the neighborhood. These two modes of response do not, as in the previous view, exist in a cause-effect relationship but are both associated with Negro residential demand. A third point of view combines these two and will be summarized in the closing paragraphs of this chapter.

The way to determine whether the association between a comparatively hostile initial response and the present proportion of Negroes is spurious would be to control for the degree of Negro demand at the time integration occurred. If, among neighborhoods in which the degree of Negro demand is similar, a hostile white response was still associated with the current proportion of Negroes in the neighborhood, we would conclude that this relationship is a genuine one. Unfortunately, our data provide a slender thread indeed on which to base this conclusion. First, as noted earlier, our measure of the Negro demand for housing postdated the time desegregation actually occurred. Second, because our two independent variables are so clearly associated with each other, the number of neighborhoods in one cell of the "minor" diagonal is very small.

Table 4.7 shows the current proportion of Negroes in northern and western neighborhoods. Each of the two independent variables has been dichotomized. The demand variable is the current distance of the neighborhood from the "nearest predominantly Negro area." The reaction variable deals with whether or not the community response was classified as one of "panic" by a majority of the neighborhood informants. The crucial comparisons are the vertical ones. We recall from Table 4.6 that Negro households comprised 10.4 percent of the neighborhoods which reacted with panic and 5.7 percent of those which did not, a difference of 4.7 percent. This difference is

Table 4.7 *Percent Negro in Neighborhood and Community Reaction to Entry of First Negroes, by Distance to Nearest Negro Segregated Neighborhood, for Northern and Western Integrated Neighborhoods (Percent Negro in Neighborhood)*

Community Reaction—Panic	Distance from Nearest Negro Segregated Neighborhood (in Miles)	
	1 or Less	*2 or More*
Yes	12.2	4.8
No	11.7	1.7

Note: The number of residents residing in the 108 neighborhoods are distributed in the cells above as follows:

219	71
577	876

Clearly the independent and control variables are associated. Over ¾ (219/290) of the residents of neighborhoods that "panicked" live one mile or less from an all-Negro area. Among those who did not live in "panic" neighborhoods, only about ⅖ (577/1,453) lived in such a neighborhood.

reduced once account is taken of the fact that the neighborhoods reacting with panic were much more likely to be one mile or less from the nearest Negro neighborhoods than are those that did not react in this manner.

Our interpretation of Table 4.7 (if we could be more sanguine about the reliability of the data) would establish a causal chain in which propinquity to a Negro neighborhood produces greater panic when the first Negro families arrive in a neighborhood, and that this reaction is translated into active behavior as whites leave the neighborhood and are replaced by Negroes. Unfortunately, this reduction of the original percentage difference does not occur when alternative measures of pressure (*e.g.*, the maximum percent Negro in the adjacent neighborhoods) or neighborhood reaction (*e.g.*, brokers encouraging whites to leave) are used. Perhaps the lack of consistency across various measures of the same concept can be attributed to the small sample size in one or another cell of the relevant tables. As it is, the figure of 4.8 percent in Table 4.7 is based on a mere six neighborhoods that were classified as reacting with panic and being two miles or more from the nearest Negro segregated neighborhood.

Earlier we considered two possible explanations for the association between a hostile white response to desegregation and the present relatively high proportion of Negroes to be found living in the neighborhood. The simpler one asserted that the association represented a genuine causal relationship where a hostile initial white response (H) creates the climate for subsequent white exodus and increased levels of Negro residency (N). It can be diagrammed thus:

$$H \longrightarrow N$$

The alternative explanation says that the association is spurious, that both these phenomena are caused by high

Negro housing demand (**D**) in the neighborhood. It can be diagrammed:

Although it is clearly going beyond the data at hand, it is probably accurate to adopt a third and more realistic perspective with respect to these issues. Negro demand probably has a dual role, affecting racial change both directly and indirectly. Directly, it produces a racial change independent of the neighborhood's particular reaction to the arrival of the first Negro family. Indirectly, demand yields racial change via the hostile response that it engenders at the time of integration. This dual role can be diagrammed:

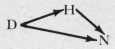

It should be pointed out that our data and this discussion refer to neighborhoods that contain fairly few Negroes and that are not changing—that is, those into which whites are currently moving. This perspective suggests that in predicting future stability for these neighborhoods or in studying changing communities, the degree of Negro demand and the inital neighborhood response are variables that cannot be ignored.

5 The Characteristics of Residents in Integrated Neighborhoods

ALTHOUGH MANY variables affect a family's decision about where to live, the critical ones are the family's social and economic status, age, size, religion, and ethnic background. In this chapter we consider each of these variables in terms of living in integrated neighborhoods.

The most important single variable is income, since a family chooses a neighborhood and dwelling only within the range of housing it can afford. As many fair-housing groups have learned, the Negro market for housing in integrated neighborhoods is limited by economic factors. An informant in an integrated neighborhood said, "We're all working hard to integrate it. We just don't seem to attract many Negro families." Another stated, "Our houses are in an upper economic level and Negroes don't have sufficient purchasing power." Conversely, an informant in a white segregated neighborhood put it this way: "They know they are safe [from integration] because the Negroes can't afford it."

Perhaps the most common criticism of social science is that it merely underscores what everyone already knows.

Although the results of our study of the socio-economic characteristics of households in integrated neighborhoods may be regarded by some as wholly predictable, we must confess that they surprised us. For example, we had expected to find only minor differences in the socio-economic levels of open, moderately integrated, and substantially integrated neighborhoods. Instead our research shows that there are major differences in socio-economic level between open and substantially integrated neighborhoods, and some small but consistent differences between open and moderately integrated neighborhoods.

The median income in open neighborhoods is higher and the median income in substantially integrated neighborhoods is lower than the median income of all households in the United States. These income differences simply reflect the major income differences between Negroes and whites in the United States. As we will show later, the cost of housing is lower in substantially integrated neighborhoods than in other integrated neighborhoods. Thus, these are the neighborhoods where a high percentage of Negroes can afford to live. Most whites who live in substantially integrated neighborhoods also do so in part because they cannot afford higher-priced housing. Nevertheless, the income levels of whites in moderately and substantially integrated neighborhoods are still higher than those of Negroes. An interesting reversal of this is seen in open neighborhoods, where we found the median income of Negro households to be higher than the median income of whites.

Since we controlled for income in selecting the white and Negro segregated neighborhoods we studied, no meaningful comparisons can be made between all integrated and all control neighborhoods. The median incomes in white segregated neighborhoods are between those in open and moderately integrated neighborhoods. The median incomes in Negro segregated neighborhoods are nearest to, but somewhat higher than, the median incomes in substantially integrated neighborhoods, since nearly all of the

Negro families in integrated neighborhoods live in substantially integrated neighborhoods. Because most integrated neighborhoods are in northern metropolitan areas where household income is higher than in rural areas and in the South, the median household income in all integrated neighborhoods combined is higher than the median household income in all segregated neighborhoods.

There are some differences in age and size of family by neighborhood type, but these differences are small compared with those due to socio-economic status—smaller than might have been predicted. White families in open neighborhoods and white segregated neighborhoods are somewhat younger and larger than families in moderately and substantially integrated neighborhoods. The head of the household in Negro families is older in open and moderately integrated neighborhoods than the head of the household in substantially integrated and Negro segregated neighborhoods. The major difference among Negroes is in type of household. About seven of eight households in open neighborhoods consist of a husband and wife, compared with about half in substantially integrated and Negro segregated neighborhoods.

Religion and ethnic background are also factors in living in integrated neighborhoods. Jews and Catholics are far more likely to live in integrated neighborhoods than Protestants. This is due in part to the regional distribution of Jews and Catholics—that is, more Jews and Catholics live in the Northeast where there are a large number of integrated neighborhoods. Prejudice against Jews and Catholics in white segregated neighborhoods may also be a reason. Many all-white neighborhoods exclude not only Negroes but also Jews and Catholics, or at least did so in the recent past.

A similar pattern is observed among ethnic groups. The earliest immigrants to the United States, the English and the Scotch, are least likely to live in integrated neighborhoods, while the most recent immigrant groups are most likely to live in integrated neighborhoods.

SOCIO-ECONOMIC CHARACTERISTICS

The socio-economic characteristics of integrated and segregated neighborhoods as measured by the distribution of household income, education of the household head, occupation of the household head, and the median Duncan socio-economic status score[1] are given in Tables 5.1 and 5.2.

The data for whites (Table 5.1) and Negroes (Table 5.2) are presented separately because there are large differences in the economic levels of the control groups. White segregated neighborhoods were sampled to match the economic levels of white residents of integrated neighborhoods; Negro segregated neighborhoods were similarly sampled to match the economic level of Negro residents of

[1] The Duncan score is based on the prestige of occupations as estimated by the average level of education and income of 1950 U. S. Census occupation categories. For a fuller explanation, see Duncan (1961).

Table 5.1 *Socio-economic Characteristics of White Households in Integrated and Segregated Neighborhoods (Percent of Households)*

Characteristic	White Segregated	Open	Moderately Integrated	Substantially Integrated	Negro Segregated	U.S. [a]
Household income (1966):						
Under $2,000	5	4	8	14	9	14
$2,000–$2,999	4	6	5	8	2	7
$3,000–$3,999	5	4	7	9	11	7
$4,000–$4,999	6	4	7	9	8	7
$5,000–$5,999	8	8	9	12	10	8
$6,000–$6,999	9	8	10	10	7	9
$7,000–$7,999	10	9	9	12	10	8
$8,000–$9,999	18	19	19	9	16	14
$10,000–$14,999	22	22	17	10	16	18
$15,000 or over	13	16	9	7	11	8
Total	100	100	100	100	100	100
N	(534)	(989)	(759)	(426)	(102)	
Median income	$8,400	$8,600	$7,500	$5,800	$7,300	$6,800

(Table 5.1 continued)

Table 5.1 *Continued*

Characteristic	Neighborhood Type					
	White Segre-gated	Open	Moder-ately Inte-grated	Sub-stan-tially Inte-grated	Negro Segre-gated	U.S.[b]
Education of household head:						
8 years or less	17	16	17	35	26	27
9–11 years	19	15	20	22	18	18
12 years	28	30	27	25	35	31
1–3 years of college	15	14	14	9	5	11
4 or more years of college	21	25	22	9	16	13
Total	100	100	100	100	100	100
N	(559)	(1,065)	(780)	(464)	(113)	
Median years	12.0	12.1	12.0	10.5	11.7	12.2
Occupation of employed household head (April 1967):						
Professional	16	19	18	8	15	
Manager	16	22	16	14	13	
Clerical—sales	13	13	11	11	9	
Craftsman	19	12	15	16	15	
Operative	12	11	10	16	17	
Other	24	23	30	35	31	
Total	100	100	100	100	100	
	(593)	(1,108)	(853)	(494)	(122)	
Median Duncan socio-economic status score	43	49	44	35	41	
N	(497)	(943)	(659)	(369)	(89)	

[a] *Source:* U.S. Bureau of the Census (1967, p. 23).

[b]*Source:* U.S. Bureau of the Census (1967, p. 27).

integrated neighborhoods. Since we selected control neighborhoods to match the income of integrated neighborhoods, the median income of the white segregated neighborhoods is $8,400, which is between the median income of open and moderately integrated neighborhoods. It is clear that white residents in substantially integrated neighborhoods cannot be compared to residents in the white segregated neighborhoods without controlling for socio-economic variables.

As has long been known, the four measures employed here are so closely correlated that it is not surprising that the differences by neighborhood type are consistent. Households in open neighborhoods consistently have the highest status and are substantially above the national average for all neighborhoods. Households in moderately integrated neighborhoods are slightly lower than open neighborhoods, but they are still above the national average. Households in substantially integrated neighborhoods are far below the open and moderately integrated areas and below the national average.

The economic level of Negro households in segregated neighborhoods is between those of Negro households in

Table 5.2 *Socio-economic Characteristics of Negro Households in Integrated and Segregated Neighborhoods (Percent of Households)*

| Characteristic | Neighborhood Type | | | | |
	Open	Moderately Integrated	Substantially Integrated	Negro Segregated	U.S.[a]
Household income (1966):					
Under $2,000	2	17	23	18	27
$2,000–$2,999	2	8	15	17	13
$3,000–$3,999	3	12	10	11	12
$4,000–$4,999	3	8	8	8	10
$5,000–$5,999	4	8	8	9	8
$6,000–$6,999	9	10	10	7	7
$7,000–$7,999	4	7	5	9	6
$8,000–$9,999	9	10	9	11	7
$10,000–$14,999	27	5	7	7	8
$15,000 or more	37	15	5	3	2
Total	100	100	100	100	100
N	(69)	(49)	(461)	(260)	
Median income	$9,000	$5,600	$4,000	$4,400	$3,800

(Table 5.2 continued)

Table 5.2 *Continued*

Characteristic	Open	Moder-ately Inte-grated	Sub-stan-tially Inte-grated	Negro Segre-gated	U.S.[b]
		Neighborhood Type			
Education of household head:					
8 years or less	11	25	42	42	45
9–11 years	14	25	24	22	23
12 years	4	22	19	21	21
1–3 years of college	14	10	9	9	6
4 or more years of college	57	18	6	6	5
Total	100	100	100	100	100
N	(69)	(49)	(451)	(231)	
Median years	16.0	11.5	9.5	9.6	9.6
Occupation of employed household head (April 1967):					
Professional	47	22	4	7	
Manager	11	6	6	3	
Clerical—sales	13	4	6	2	
Craftsman	6	20	12	13	
Operative	11	6	19	22	
Service	4	13	17	22	
Other	8	29	36	31	
Total	100	100	100	100	
N	(69)	(49)	(494)	(278)	
Median Duncan socio-economic status score	67	44	18	16	
N	(69)	(49)	(493)	(278)	

[a] *Source:* U.S. Bureau of the Census (1967, p. 23).

[b] *Source:* U.S. Bureau of the Census (1967, p. 28).

moderately and substantially integrated neighborhoods. Negro residents of open neighborhoods, whose economic levels are more comparable to those of whites in these neighborhoods, cannot be compared to the Negro control group without controlling for socio-economic variables.

SOCIO-ECONOMIC DIFFERENCES BY
NEIGHBORHOOD TYPE

Since the types of neighborhoods we studied are not all communities in the same size of place or in the same geographic region and since a neighborhood's socio-economic status is influenced by these factors, the socio-economic differences among types of integrated neighborhoods might be expected to disappear when region, size of place, or other factors are controlled. We found, however, that controlling for region, size of place. and urbanization does not reduce the differences between income levels of open, moderately integrated, and substantially integrated neighborhoods, nor does controlling for ownership status or number of full-time earners. The number of full-time earners, however, may explain why in open neighborhoods Negro households have higher median incomes than white households. In the small sample of Negro households in open neighborhoods, a higher percentage of both husbands and wives worked than in white households.

Although the income differences between owners and renters do not explain differences in the median incomes of integrated and segregated neighborhoods, we shall see later that the percentages of owners and renters vary in these neighborhoods, but these variations are effects rather than causes of income differences. If none of these variables explains the differences in socio-economic level by type of neighborhood, then what is the reason? It is, to put it quite simply, due to the fact that whites currently earn more money than Negroes.

In the past—if not currently—it has been the general policy of real estate builders and sellers, as well as of the United States government as expressed in the Federal Housing Administration (FHA) mortgage provisions, that neighborhoods should be economically homogeneous. For this reason, even if there were no racial discrimination in housing, those neighborhoods that had a higher proportion of Negroes would generally have poorer whites. The differences in the income distributions between the two races are well known.

There are still very few Negroes in America who can afford expensive housing. The median income for Negro families and unrelated individuals was $3,800 in 1966, compared with $6,800 for whites. We do not say, nor do we believe, that there is no housing discrimination. Most remaining white segregated neighborhoods still have substantial barriers to prevent Negroes from moving in, even if the Negroes are economically qualified. What we are saying is that, even if all these barriers disappeared through legal action or changes in public opinion, there would still be severe economic barriers facing most Negroes who wished to live in open and moderately integrated neighborhoods.

This conclusion is a sharp reminder that attitudes play a secondary role to economics in the housing market. The white residents of substantially integrated neighborhoods live there mainly because they cannot afford to move elsewhere. They are not more likely to be pro-integration than residents of open and moderately integrated neighborhoods are, but indeed, as will be shown later, they are more likely to share the anti-Negro attitudes of white residents of changing neighborhoods than the attitudes of the higher-income whites in open and moderately integrated neighborhoods, who have a wider range of choices available to them.

RELIGION

Table 5.3 shows some important religious differences among the white households in integrated neighborhoods and in segregated neighborhoods. Perhaps the most striking difference is in the percentage of Jews. Only 1 percent of the white households in segregated neighborhoods are Jewish, compared with 9 percent in open neighborhoods, and about 5 percent each in moderately and substantially integrated and Negro segregated neigh-

Table 5.3 *Religious Affiliation of White Households in Integrated and Segregated Neighborhoods (Percent of Households)*

Religious Affiliation	Neighborhood Type				
	White Segregated	Open	Moderately Integrated	Substantially Integrated	Negro Segregated
Protestant	47	28	34	39	36
Baptist	13	5	5	20	9
Methodist	12	6	6	6	5
Lutheran	6	4	5	3	5
Presbyterian	4	4	7	3	8
Episcopalian	3	2	5	2	3
United Church of Christ	4	4	2	1	4
Other Protestant	5	3	4	4	2
Catholic	35	44	38	41	37
Jewish	1	9	6	4	6
Other religion	4	3	2	1	2
No religious affiliation	13	16	20	15	19
Total	100	100	100	100	100

borhoods. These figures indicate not only a greater probability of Jews living in integrated neighborhoods, but possibly also the fact that Jews are not or were not welcome in many neighborhoods that have no Negroes.

The proportion of Roman Catholics is also about 10 percentage points higher in open than in segregated neighborhoods, but part of this difference is explained by regional variation. In the South and West, where Catholics are a minority, the proportion of Catholics is higher in integrated than in segregated neighborhoods. The reverse is the case in the Northeast, where Catholics are a majority, but some of this may be due to the households who claim no religious affiliation. In the Northeast, where most Jews live, the differences between open and white segregated neighborhoods are even more striking than they are nationally. Only 1 percent of Jews live in white segregated neighborhoods, compared with 13 percent in open neighborhoods. In all regions, the proportion of Protestants is higher in white segregated than in integrated neighborhoods.

Among Negroes the pattern is quite similar. The Negroes living in integrated neighborhoods are more likely to be Catholic than those in Negro segregated neighborhoods. This difference is particularly striking in the South, where 20 percent of the Negroes in substantially integrated neighborhoods are Catholic, while only about 2 percent of the Negroes in segregated neighborhoods are Catholic.

The religion of residents was determined by finding out what church they now attend most frequently. The percentage claiming some religious affiliation is highest among Negroes in Negro segregated neighborhoods and among whites in white segregated neighborhoods.

ETHNIC BACKGROUND

The daily news reports generally stress the conflicts that occur between Negroes and those ethnic groups which have immigrated to the United States most recently, while WASP's (white, Anglo-Saxon Protestants) do not have the same kinds of public conflicts that make news. The results of our study are thus surprising. We find that for the most recently arrived ethnic groups—the Italians, French, Poles, Russians, and other Eastern Europeans—the percentage of households is higher in integrated than in segregated neighborhoods. Conversely, there is a higher percentage of WASP's in segregated than in integrated neighborhoods.

Further reflection suggests, however, that public conflict between the newer ethnic groups and Negroes exists because they are in competition for the same housing as well as for economic and political power. In some neighborhoods, particularly substantially integrated ones, this competition has led to a stable equilibrium, at least for the foreseeable future, regardless of the attitudes of white residents toward integration. In other areas, these conflicts have led to changing neighborhoods. Nevertheless, by extrapolation, it appears more likely that Negroes will in the future be living among Poles and Italians than among Englishmen and Scots.

POLICY IMPLICATIONS

The wide differences in income levels between Negroes and whites, given the current tendency toward economic homogeneity of almost all neighborhoods, limit the number of Negroes in open and moderately integrated neighborhoods even if more whites and Negroes are willing to live next door to each other. In the recent past, it was impossible for middle- and upper-class Negroes to live in integrated areas, even if they could afford it. As these restrictions are removed, economic barriers become increasingly important, as indicated by the many suburban fair-housing groups that search without success for Negro families to move in and integrate their communities.

Obviously, one way of breaking down economic barriers is to increase the number of middle-class Negroes. Programs must be created that will make it possible for more Negroes to attend college and enter the professions; to work in skilled, technical jobs, and in the crafts; and to start businesses of their own. The need for such programs has been emphasized more intensely by the Urban League and other black civil rights activists than by white fair-housing groups. Yet, it is clear that any effort to enact fair-housing laws and to attract even a few Negroes into previously all-white neighborhoods will largely be wasted if there are not enough Negro middle-class families who can afford to make the move.

6 *Variety Is the Spice*

I have often amused myself with thinking how different a place London is to different people. They, whose narrow minds are contracted to the consideration of some one particular pursuit, view it only through that medium. . . . But the intellectual man is struck with it, as comprehending the whole of human life in all its variety, the contemplation of which is inexhaustible.

James Boswell (as quoted by
Jane Jacobs, 1961, p. 143)

This is a heterogeneous neighborhood in terms of what people do and their ages. There are young families with small children and families with older children away from home. Some have small businesses, many work for the government, and they all travel in different directions to their work, and this makes for a harmonious group. Just as the company town has fallen into disrepute, a diversity of employment, schools, and churches makes for harmony. There are no social pressures, nobody has to do anything.

The people here are friendly, not nosey, helpful, never intrusive. All ages—that is very important. Young and old—not everybody the same. They are bright, intellectual, "with it,"—hate subdivisions.
Residents of integrated neighborhoods

THE RESIDENTS OF integrated neighborhoods come from more widely varied religious, ethnic, economic, and educational backgrounds than the residents of white segregated neighborhoods. The reason for the higher variety is not the same for all integrated neighborhoods. Three explanations are possible:

1. Residents of integrated neighborhoods are attracted to the variety in the neighborhood.

99

2. Residents of white segregated neighborhoods prefer homogeneity, while residents of integrated neighborhoods are indifferent to it.

3. Variety, *per se*, is not an important reason for selecting a neighborhood, but is related to other factors that are important.

In order to try to establish any one of these explanations as the basis for the variety in a given neighborhood we first estimated the variety of the neighborhoods from census data and resident characteristics. Then we asked the residents about their perceptions of the variety in their neighborhoods and whether they preferred their neighbors to be the same or different.

In neighborhoods where variety was high but not perceived by the residents, we would argue that variety, *per se*, was unimportant. In neighborhoods where high variety was perceived but no sentiment for heterogeneity existed, we would characterize the residents as indifferent (but not opposed) to differences among neighbors. Finally, where high variety was both perceived and preferred—as was the case with a minority of residents—we would conclude that these residents were in fact attracted to variety for its own sake.

The results of our study suggest that residents of open and moderately integrated neighborhoods prefer, or at least do not fear, diversity among their neighbors. In other words, the willingness of whites and Negroes to live together reflects a more general willingness to relate to people of all kinds. A resident in one of these neighborhoods summed it up this way:

> We live in a world where all kinds of people live. The easiest way to teach your children to live with these different kinds is to live in a neighborhood where all kinds live.

In substantially integrated neighborhoods, however, we see no preference for variety. Residents of these neighborhoods live there mainly because they are unable to afford housing elsewhere or because they have always lived there. Curiously, although these neighborhoods may be extremely diverse in many respects, the residents still think of their neighborhoods as homogeneous.

These conclusions are necessarily general and only indications of tendencies; they do not hold, of course, for every resident of a neighborhood. As we have pointed out in earlier chapters, economic factors and housing needs play primary roles in the selection of a neighborhood. The integration of the community and variety among neighbors are secondary factors. Within segregated neighborhoods there will be some people who prefer variety but have chosen to live there because other factors are even more important. In integrated neighborhoods, conversely, there will be a substantial number of residents who dislike variety. It is clear, however, that, in the main, residents of integrated neighborhoods do not reject variety as do most residents of white segregated neighborhoods.

RELIGIOUS VARIETY

Earlier we observed that there were higher percentages of Catholics and Jews in integrated neighborhoods, but this information gives no indication of how much religious variety there is in specific neighborhoods. It might be that the Catholics or Jews live in mainly all-Catholic or all-Jewish neighborhoods. This, however, is not the case—neighborhoods where the largest religious group was 70 percent or more of the total population were classified as having low religious variety; those where the largest religious group was 51–69 percent of the population were classified as having medium religious variety; and those where the largest religious group was less than half of the population were classified as having high religious variety.

One of the striking differences between white segregated and open and moderately integrated neighborhoods is that the integrated neighborhoods show higher religious variety. If there is a connection between willingness to live in an integrated neighborhood and a liking for variety, then moderately integrated neighborhoods should have higher religious variety than open neighborhoods. Fifty-four percent of the residents of moderately integrated neighborhoods live in neighborhoods with high religious variety, compared with 42 percent of the residents of open neighborhoods and 22 percent of the residents of white segregated neighborhoods.

Religious variety is considerably higher in central cities of metropolitan areas than in suburbs; and the greatest differences between integrated and white segregated neighborhoods are found in central cities. In nonmetropolitan areas integrated neighborhoods exhibit more variety than segregated ones. The same pattern prevails in all regions except the West. Evidently, the variety of religions is so great in California that just about everyone lives in a neighborhood with high religious variety.

The religious affiliation of residents of substantially integrated neighborhoods is not as indicative of preference as it is in other neighborhoods. The choice of variety or homogeneity requires the economic means to implement that choice. As we have already pointed out, residents of substantially integrated neighborhoods are usually there because they can afford the housing in these neighborhoods. Religious variety in substantially integrated northern neighborhoods, therefore, is probably due to the fact that the Negro residents of these neighborhoods are usually Protestant while the whites are more likely to be Catholic.

ETHNIC VARIETY

Ethnic variety is measured in the same way as religious variety: the higher the proportion of the neighborhood accounted for by the largest ethnic group, the lower the ethnic variety. Neighborhoods with half or more of the residents having the same ethnicity were classified as having low ethnic variety; those with 40–49 percent of the residents in the highest ethnic group were classified as having medium ethnic variety; and those with less than 40 percent in the highest ethnic group were classified as having high ethnic variety.

The greatest variety is seen in moderately integrated neighborhoods, with white segregated neighborhoods having the least variety. The differences here are smaller than those among neighborhood types for religious variety, and this may be due to the fact that the boundaries between various ethnic groups are not as sharp as those between religions. Sixty-four percent of the residents of moderately integrated neighborhoods live in neighborhoods with high ethnic variety, compared with 54 percent of the residents of open neighborhoods and 48 percent of the residents of white segregated neighborhoods.

SOCIO-ECONOMIC VARIETY

If liking for, or less fear of, variety is a characteristic of residents of integrated neighborhoods, one would expect that these neighborhoods would show greater variety on socio-economic characteristics—particularly income and education—as well as in religion and ethnicity, and this is generally the case. The differences between integrated and white segregated neighborhoods are smaller, however, and in some cases vanish entirely.

Moderately integrated neighborhoods are more variable in income and education of household head than white segregated neighborhoods. In the latter, 63 percent of residents live in neighborhoods with low variety in income, compared with 50 percent of residents of moderately integrated neighborhoods. Also, 59 percent of residents of white segregated neighborhoods live in neighborhoods with low variety in education of household head, compared with 44 percent of residents of moderately integrated neighborhoods.

BARRIERS TO VARIETY

Most people, even those who live in integrated neighborhoods, prefer to live in homogeneous surroundings. There are many reasons for this. Given any choice in the matter, most people prefer their social contacts to be with others of the same social class and ethnic background, with whom they are more likely to share similar views on such neighborhood concerns as adequate schools and political representation. Even that minority of residents who prefer or are not afraid of heterogeneity do not wish to live in neighborhoods where no one shares their outlook on life. Such people are less concerned with background than with behavior. This majority preference for homogeneity has been institutionalized by mortgage and real estate groups and by the past policies of the Federal Housing Administration (FHA) in making mortgage insurance funds available. Thus, to quote from the FHA *Underwriting Manual* (as cited by Grier and Grier, 1966):

> If a neighborhood is to retain stability, it is necessary that properties shall continue to be occupied by the same social and racial group.

The FHA did not invent this policy; it took it over from the real estate groups it served. The earlier effects were primarily aimed against Negroes as Abrams (1966) has pointed out:

> . . . the federal government, during the New Deal period, not only sanctioned racial discrimination in housing but vigorously exhorted it. From 1935 to 1950, discrimination against Negroes was a condition of federal assistance. More than 11 million homes were built during this period, and this federal policy did more to entrench housing bias in American neighborhoods than any court could undo by a ruling. It established federally sponsored mores for discrimination in suburban communities in which 80 percent of all new housing is being built and fixed the social and racial patterns in thousands of new neighborhoods.

Although today the official federal policy is open housing for all races, religions, and ethnic groups, earlier
policies in effect during the post–World War II building
boom established areas that still retain their original
homogeneous character. With few exceptions, current real
estate and mortgage policies continue to encourage economic homogeneity. A family that wanted to live in a
neighborhood where housing values were varied would
have great difficulty in finding such a neighborhood.
Indeed, this same policy of economic homogeneity remains
one of the major barriers to integrated housing.

If integration is a national goal, the economic diversity
of neighborhoods ought to be encouraged rather than discouraged by governmental actions. At the federal level,
this could be done most effectively by revising the
financing practices of the Department of Housing and
Urban Development. At the local level, zoning could be
made sufficiently flexible to permit good houses of all
kinds, sizes, and values to be built in the same neighborhood. Fair-housing groups may play a major role in
developing public and governmental attitudes that are
more hospitable to the creation of such varied neighborhoods.

Although they may not yet constitute a majority of the
country, there are still a large number of Americans who
find ethnic, religious, and racial variety to be the spice of
life. Many of these people would enjoy similar economic
variety in their neighborhoods.

Much of the preference for economic homogeneity is
based on the fear that heterogeneity in a neighborhood
automatically lowers property values. This fear is not irra-
tional when supported by government actions that rein-
force it. Yet, as in the case of integrated neighborhoods,
there is no intrinsic reason why variety must cause property values to go down. Changes in behavior by federal and
local governmental housing agencies should make it possible to develop economically heterogeneous neighborhoods for those who want them.

7 *The Characteristics of Housing and the Housing Market*

SINCE HOUSING choice is so dependent on available income, the characteristics of housing in integrated and segregated neighborhoods are directly related to the socio-economic conditions in these neighborhoods. There are many people who believe, in spite of all evidence to the contrary, that property values go down when an area becomes integrated. In their studies, Laurenti (1960) and others found, after controlling for social class, that housing values do not depreciate as a result of integration. It is true that substantially integrated neighborhoods have lower-priced housing than open and white segregated neighborhoods, but this is probably a cause rather than an effect of integration. In other words the cost of housing in substantially integrated neighborhoods was originally low enough to make it economically possible for Negroes to move in.

It is important to remember that this is not a study of changing neighborhoods but of stable integrated neighborhoods. If a neighborhood panics when Negroes move in and a large number of residents put their houses on the market simultaneously, the sudden increase in available houses certainly can cause prices to go down, at least until there are fewer houses on the market. This process can be accelerated if block-busters are working in the community. In the stable integrated neighborhoods that we studied, we found very little evidence of even short-term depressions in the cost of housing when the first Negroes moved in.

A point worth noting about integration is that white segregated neighborhoods are likely to have been developed by a single builder. Initially, then, it is easier to keep a neighborhood closed to Negroes when there is only a single source of supply. Attitude toward variety also may be a contributing factor. Houses of a single builder are very similar in style and size and, thus, appeal to buyers who prefer homogeneity.

OWNERS AND RENTERS

Although the housing values are about the same in both integrated and segregated neighborhoods, the kinds of housing in these neighborhoods differ. The differences are large enough to shed some light on the long-standing argument about how renting versus owning affects integration. On the one hand, it has been argued that it is very hard to integrate rental housing because it is so easy for white tenants to move out if Negroes move in. The opposing view is that, since white tenants do not have to worry about property values and are less likely to associate closely with other neighborhood residents, they probably will stay. However, differences are not entirely due to white renters' attitudes. The income distribution of Negro households is a major factor. Given their lower incomes and the great difficulty they have in obtaining mortgages, Negro families are more likely to rent than to own their homes.

The results of our study indicate that there is a higher proportion of renters in integrated areas than elsewhere in the United States, while in white and Negro segregated neighborhoods the proportion of homeowners is higher than the national average. Fifty-six percent of the residents of moderately integrated neighborhoods and 61 percent of the residents of open neighborhoods are homeowners, compared with 73 percent of the residents of white segregated neighborhoods. (The national average at the time of our study, 1967, was about 64 percent.) These proportional differences exist in each region and type of place with one exception. In the suburbs of metropolitan areas, about 80 percent of the residents of both white segregated and open neighborhoods are owners, but even there the percentage of owners in moderately integrated neighborhoods is lower (71 percent). The most extreme differences are observed in the central cities of the largest metropolitan areas, where 40 to 45 percent of the residents of open and moderately integrated neighborhoods are owners, while 61 percent of the residents of white segregated neighborhoods are owners.

The same sort of differences show up when we compare substantially integrated neighborhoods with Negro segregated neighborhoods. Although the differences are not quite as great as in the other neighborhoods, they are consistent by region except in the South, which shows the effect of different historical patterns.

The largest observed difference in the extent of home owning is between whites and Negroes in substantially integrated neighborhoods. About two-thirds of all whites, but less than half of all Negroes, own their homes. Although this may be explained in part by the difference in median incomes ($5,800 for white households, $4,000 for Negro households), the inability of Negro families to obtain home financing is also an important factor.

Among Negroes in central cities of metropolitan areas there are more renters in substantially integrated than in segregated neighborhoods, but in suburban areas the number of homeowners is the same in these two types of neighborhoods. Among whites, the proportion of renters is higher in suburban substantially integrated neighborhoods than in suburban Negro segregated neighborhoods. In central cities, however, the pattern is reversed: the proportion of white renters is higher in the Negro segregated neighborhoods. Although the proportion of renters is higher in integrated than in white segregated neighborhoods, the majority of white residents in all kinds of integrated neighborhoods are homeowners. Only among Negroes in substantially integrated neighborhoods are renters a majority.

These complex patterns result from various forces. First, given the inequity of income distribution between Negroes and whites, it is harder for Negroes to buy than to rent. Therefore, there will be more Negroes in the market for housing in neighborhoods that contain both rental and owner-occupied units than in neighborhoods without rental units. Second, white renters are not as sensitive as white owners to the presence of a low proportion of Negroes in the neighborhood. Renters are less likely to come in close contact with their neighbors, and many white renters are probably unaware that there are Negroes in the neighborhood. Renters, moreover, do not have any particular fears about property values declining. Third, many rental units are managed by agents who represent absentee owners or trusts. Therefore, relatively few agents or management companies can open a considerable number of rental units to Negroes. Thus, the combination of these forces makes it easier to integrate a white segregated neighborhood if it has some rental units.

On the other hand, a changing neighborhood with many rental units is likely to become Negro segregated. If the neighborhood is located near other Negro segregated neighborhoods and therefore under pressure from the expanding Negro ghetto, the same forces that operated to integrate white segregated neighborhoods will operate to segregate the changing neighborhood. Renters have greater mobility than homeowners because they have the advantage of being able to move out of a neighborhood more quickly than owners, who often must wait until they sell their property. Since renters are usually not deeply involved in neighborhood activities and know fewer residents, they do not hesitate to leave a neighborhood. Ultimately, then, the vacancies left by white renters are filled by Negroes who can afford the rentals.

HOUSING VALUES

In this section we compare the values and conditions of Negro and white housing in integrated and segregated neighborhoods. Our conclusions are at best tentative for two reasons. Although owners of single-family homes cannot assess perfectly the value of their homes, we use owners' estimates because we consider them more accurate than estimates based on 1960 census data, current monthly mortgage payments, or the cost of the home when it was purchased. Secondly, our analysis of housing conditions is not exhaustive, since the only features it includes are the number of bedrooms and bathrooms; the availability of garages or parking facilities; and, for renters, the quality of janitorial services. Among the features that are excluded are size and arrangement of rooms, fixtures, and heating and ventilation.

In discussing our findings, we separate the high-income neighborhoods—white segregated, open, and moderately integrated—from the low-income neighborhoods—substantially integrated and Negro segregated.

High-income Neighborhoods

The results of our investigation indicate that, for homeowners in the high-income neighborhoods, housing quality is closely related to price with no differences between integrated and white segregated neighborhoods—that is, one pays neither more nor less for living in an open or moderately integrated neighborhood. Perceived housing value is highest in open neighborhoods, where the median value of a home is $22,000. In white segregated and moderately integrated neighborhoods values are slightly lower, the median value being $19,000. These differences correspond to the differences in the neighborhoods' income distributions, indicating that income is highest in open neighborhoods.

For renters, the median rent is not the same in open, moderately integrated, and white segregated neighborhoods. In white segregated neighborhoods the median rent is $82 per month, an amount substantially below that of the $96 per month median in moderately integrated neighborhoods, and far below the $111 per month in open neighborhoods. Again, income distribution accounts for the difference between open and moderately integrated neighborhoods.

In white segregated neighborhoods, it is possible that the low median rent is the result of variability in our sampling. The figure is based on a smaller sample of residents than the other figures because fewer than 30 percent of the residents in these neighborhoods are renters.

There are, moreover, no meaningful differences in the quality of rental housing in white segregated, open, and moderately integrated neighborhoods. The median number of bedrooms is 1.8 in white segregated and in open neighborhoods, and 1.7 in moderately integrated ones. Renters in white segregated neighborhoods are more likely to have parking facilities than renters in integrated neighborhoods, but they are also more likely to be dissatisfied with their janitorial service.

Controlling for region, city size, urbanization, and age of structure fails to explain why white segregated neighborhoods have a lower median rent than integrated neighborhoods, but the median rent is consistently lower. Simple economics provides the best explanation. Given a fixed supply of a commodity—in this case, rental units—the price will tend to increase as the market expands. In open and moderately integrated neighborhoods, where rental units are available to both Negroes and whites, there will be a larger market for rental units. With this increased demand, the rents will be higher than for comparable housing in white segregated neighborhoods, where the market is restricted to whites. The irony is, because of discrimination, Negroes have both little chance of owning a house and few alternatives in the rental market and, hence, are often compelled to pay higher rents. Thus, landlords who discriminate against Negroes pay a penalty for doing so, while white renters receive a premium in lower rents.

Low-income Neighborhoods

There are no differences of any consequence in the condition of housing among Negroes, whether they be homeowners or renters, between substantially integrated and Negro segregated neighborhoods. However, rents, housing values, and the quality of the housing in these neighborhoods are in general considerably below those in white segregated, open, and moderately integrated neighborhoods, reflecting the differing income distributions. The houses of low-income neighborhood homeowners have, on the average, fewer bedrooms and bathrooms than those of high-income neighborhood homeowners. The same conditions exist for renters in low-income neighborhoods except that, since apartments in these neighborhoods are generally older and larger than apartments in high-income neighborhoods, they have more bedrooms.

Although white rental housing is about the same in both substantially integrated and Negro segregated neighborhoods, there are interesting differences between the housing of white homeowners in each of these types of neighborhoods. Any conclusions, however, about the cause of these differences are highly speculative, because the number of white households in Negro segregated neighborhoods is so small, particularly after owners are separated from renters. Among white owners in substantially integrated neighborhoods, the median value of housing is only $12,000; while in Negro segregated neighborhoods it is $21,000, which is not only considerably higher than in substantially integrated neighborhoods but also higher than in all neighborhoods except the open integrated ones.

This suggests that white owners in Negro segregated neighborhoods value their property more highly than owners in other neighborhoods, which may help to explain why they are still living in these neighborhoods. It is interesting to speculate, but we have no way of knowing whether the high valuations of property in Negro segregated neighborhoods are causes or effects of the neighborhood's change, or are related to other, more basic variables.

HOUSING-VALUE JUDGMENTS

We asked both residents and informants the following question about the value of the housing in their neighborhoods:

Considering both price and quality, how would you rate the housing value in this neighborhood—that is, what you get for your money? Is it over-priced, about right, or is it a particularly good value?

We also asked our informants to rate the housing in their neighborhoods "compared to other neighborhoods in the metropolitan area/county."

We were not surprised to find that, overall, renters are more likely than owners to think that housing is overpriced, since for renters housing is only an expense while for owners it is also an investment. Not so obvious is the feeling of Negro owners and renters that housing in their neighborhoods is overpriced.

In substantially integrated neighborhoods Negro owners perceive their own homes as being worth about the same as those owned by their white neighbors. Furthermore, in substantially integrated neighborhoods neither the rents paid by Negroes or whites nor the number of bedrooms in either owned or rented housing are significantly different, though there are some differences in the number of bathrooms and in parking facilities for Negroes and whites. Thirty-five percent of the white homeowners as compared with only 14 percent of the Negro homeowners have two or more bathrooms, and white owners and renters are more likely to have parking facilities than Negro owners and renters. We believe that these conditions account for only a small part of the difference between Negro and white housing-value judgments. Negro reactions to white discrimination and general Negro attitudes toward whites may also be responsible.

Perhaps an even more important factor is the percentage of disposable income spent on housing. When one compares median incomes, housing values, and rental payments, it is clear that in general Negroes spend a higher proportion of their income on housing than whites. Thus, what Negro respondents may really be saying is that they spend too high a percentage of their total income on housing, rather than that the absolute amount paid is too high. We have not developed a measure of the percentage of income spent on housing for individual households. Although this would be easy to do for renters, it would be extremely difficult for homeowners because it would involve notions of alternative sources of investment of funds that are far beyond the scope of this study.

Among owners in all of the high-income neighborhoods, the value judgments do not vary greatly. Renters in open and moderately integrated neighborhoods are more likely to think that their housing is overpriced than renters in white segregated neighborhoods; reported median rents support this view. This judgment probably reflects the fact that, when rental units are available to both races, the market and demand for them increase so that higher rents may be obtained.

The housing-value judgments of white and Negro owners and renters in substantially integrated and Negro segregated neighborhoods (the low-income neighborhoods) are based on rather small samples so our conclusions must be considered tentative. They do, nevertheless, generally confirm what one might expect: among both white owners and renters, housing is more likely to be considered overpriced in substantially integrated than in Negro segregated neighborhoods. This is what the supply-demand equilibrium would suggest since the supply in substantially integrated neighborhoods is small and the market large.

Among Negroes in the low-income neighborhoods, the housing-value judgments are reversed. Negro owners and renters in substantially integrated areas think that housing is a particularly good value. This judgment cannot be explained on the basis of economic factors. A possible answer is that Negroes living in integrated areas will be more likely to associate more closely with their white neighbors, and thus their judgments of housing values will be more similiar to those of the whites.

THE CURRENT HOUSING MARKET

This section discusses residents' and informants' judgments about the current housing markets in their neighborhoods. To obtain this information we asked two questions: "When a house is up for sale at the going price, does it generally get sold in less than a month, one to three months, four to six months, or more than six months?" and "Are there many vacant apartments in this neighborhood, are there only a few, or is there a waiting list?"

According to informants, within high-income neighborhoods the housing markets differ in two respects. First, there are more rental units with waiting lists in open neighborhoods than in white segregated neighborhoods. Second, as the proportion of Negro residents rises in the neighborhood, according to informants, it takes longer to sell houses. The first difference can be explained by the fact that in open and in moderately integrated neighborhoods, there is a greater demand for rental units than in white segregated neighborhoods. The second difference is not as easily explained. It is not clear whether the difference is a cause or an effect. In other words, it may be that, when houses become harder to sell to whites, owners are more willing to sell to Negroes. On the other hand, as the proportion of Negroes increases, it may be harder to find white buyers, even though some still buy and the area remains integrated.

Negroes have greater difficulty in financing their houses than whites. Whether this is due to racial prejudice or to the overall lower income levels of Negro families, one thing is clear: the problem of selling houses to Negroes is often that it takes longer for the deals to go through, and a higher proportion simply fall through because financing cannot be obtained.

A comparison of substantially integrated neighborhoods and Negro segregated neighborhoods indicates that it is easier for Negroes to obtain conventional financing in an all-Negro neighborhood than in a substantially integrated one. The same is true for whites in substantially integrated and Negro segregated neighborhoods, but here the situation is muddied by economic differences.

POLICY IMPLICATIONS

Major increases in integration may be achieved by opening segregated rental units to Negroes. Not only does this benefit the Negro renter, but the owner of the apartment building also benefits by increasing the demand for his apartments. In the long run, he makes more money, either by increased rents or by reducing the number of vacancies.

The increase in rental units also lowers the housing demands that Negroes make on substantially integrated neighborhoods, which would make it easier for these neighborhoods to remain stable. Moreover, as more and more areas are integrated, the ability of renters to move to segregated neighborhoods is reduced, so there is less reason for them to move. It is highly unlikely that in neighborhoods far from the Negro ghetto the presence of some Negro renters will radically affect the stability of the neighborhood.

Since discrimination in rental housing is now generally illegal, the expectation is that both government and private fair-housing groups will apply continuous pressure on landlords to desegregate their units. Although the task of first proving discrimination and then removing it is not easy, it is nonetheless clearly worth the effort for it could pay off in a substantial increase in the number of integrated rental units.

There are likely to be many more Negro renters than buyers who are willing to be pioneers in white segregated neighborhoods. The problem is with the landlords. At present, most fair-housing groups appear to have concentrated their energies on attracting Negro buyers to upper-middle-class suburbs. It is probably more productive for these groups to work with landlords than to search for Negro families who can afford an expensive home in the suburbs.

8 *Attitudes Toward Integration*

OVER THE PAST twenty-five years, the only period for which there is even moderately reliable data on public attitudes toward integration, there has been a consistent trend toward greater white acceptance of equality for Negroes—including greater acceptance of residential integration. For example, in 1942 only slightly more than one-third of the whites in the United States said that it would make no difference to them if a Negro with the same income and education moved onto their block. By 1956 this figure had risen to slightly over one-half, and by 1965 approximately two-thirds had come to view the possibility of a Negro moving onto their block with (at least verbal) equanimity (Schwartz, 1967). In the available data that provide a basis for comparison over time, we see similarly favorable trends in other white attitudes toward Negroes.

While data on the number of integrated neighborhoods do not in and of themselves tell us if there have been like trends in behavior, the general evidence suggests that the country is making some slow progress toward increasing residential integration. The relation between attitudes and behavior is a complex one for which there is no completely adequate theory at present. Students of social change agree that attitudes and behavior tend to be roughly consistent with one another, although everyone recognizes many instances in which attitudes and behavior do not coincide. Thus, no one would predict one-to-one correspondence between a person's attitudes and his behavior.

Traditionally most social psychologists have worked on the implicit assumption that attitudes exist prior to action and, more often than not, are causes of action. The practical implication of such an assumption is that an effective way to change someone's behavior is to change his attitudes. Thus, if, by some clever persuasion campaign, a person's attitudes could be changed, there would follow a significant increase in the likelihood that his behavior would change to accord with his new attitudes.

The psychologist's view of the relation between attitudes and behavior is widely shared by laymen. Indeed, it underlies the familiar arguments against open-housing legislation, equal-employment acts, and a variety of civil rights measures that provide legal sanctions to enforce equality of opportunity. One argument against these types of laws has been that one cannot legislate a social change in advance of a basic change in attitude and that the laws cannot be enforced until people's attitudes have changed. Implicit in this argument, of course, is the notion that, once the attitudes have changed, there will be no need for the legislation. More recently, however, Leon Festinger and his students have shown that in many instances induced behavioral change that runs counter to one's attitudes may be one of the strongest motives changing former attitudes. In this case, when one's behavior is no longer consistent with one's attitudes, the latter are changed to be in line with one's new actions.

ATTITUDES OF WHITE RESIDENTS

Over the past twenty-five years, NORC has collected

data on white attitudes toward Negroes. During that time a number of tests have shown a consistent ability to discriminate between people with more and people with less favorable attitudes toward Negroes. For this study, we used seven items that have in the past been good indicators of general integration sentiment. Table 8.1 presents the distribution of responses to each item by our neighborhood types and for the nationwide sample from the NORC study of December 1963. In addition, the table gives the distributions for four of the items from a nationwide sample taken in May 1968, shortly after the assassination of Dr. Martin Luther King, Jr.

In assessing the meaning of this table, we should first note that the attitude items fall roughly into two groups: those pertaining to equal access for Negroes to public facilities, and those pertaining to closer interpersonal association between Negroes and whites, including living in the same neighborhood. The table shows that, in the nation as a whole, a majority of whites endorse items suggesting that Negroes should have equal access to the more public areas of life. While the size of the majority differs among items, it is clear that majority opinion clearly supports equality of opportunity.

In those areas involving closer interpersonal association between Negroes and whites, such as entertaining Negroes in one's home, legal sanctions against intermarriage, and beliefs in the right to segregated residence, whites are clearly less favorable to integration. There is, moreover, slight evidence that, at least as far as private association is concerned, whites may be reversing the general trend of attitude change. In the 1968 survey, as compared with the one taken in 1963, a lower proportion of white respondents endorsed items related to housing desegregation. Further work will have to be done, however, to establish the findings of a definite reversal in the historic trend.

White residents' attitudes toward integration are somewhat out of character when compared with current behav-

Table 8.1 Distribution of Attitudes Toward Integration, by Neighborhood Type and for Total U.S. (Percent of White Residents Favorable to Integration)

Attitude Toward Integration	Neighborhood Type					Total U.S.	
	White Segregated	Open	Moderately Integrated	Substantially Integrated	Negro Segregated	1963[a]	1968[b]
Separate sections in streetcars and buses (No)	86	92	93	68	76	77	—[c]
Negroes should have same rights to use parks, restaurants, hotels, etc. (Yes)	83	92	91	65	73	71	—
Negroes should go to same schools as whites (Yes)	75	88	87	52	75	63	60
Object if family member brought Negro friend to dinner (Not at all)	59	73	67	41	54	49	—
There should be laws against interracial marriage (No)	40	56	52	26	35	36	37
White people have a right to keep Negroes out of their neighborhood (Disagree slightly or strongly)	36	40	46	26	36	44	36
Negroes shouldn't push themselves where they're not wanted (Disagree slightly or strongly)	16	23	22	12	12	27	18
N	(584)	(1,108)	(864)	(492)	(108)	(1,230)	(1,482)

[a] Source: NORC Study SRS 330, December, 1963.
[b] Source: NORC Study 4050, May, 1968.
[c] Not asked on this study.

ior. Residents of open and moderately integrated neighborhoods are more favorable to Negro rights than residents of white segregated neighborhoods. The difference between the two groups is particularly marked with respect to entertaining Negroes in the home and laws against intermarriage.

On the other hand, white residents of substantially integrated and Negro segregated neighborhoods are considerably less favorably disposed toward integration than white residents of either open or moderately integrated neighborhoods and, in some respects, have even less favorable attitudes than whites in white segregated neighborhoods. The integration attitudes of the whites living in Negro segregated neighborhoods are perhaps not difficult to understand. In some of these areas, the whites feel that they are being pushed out by the Negroes. They may be particularly resentful because of what they see as a failure by their white neighbors to hold the line and keep Negroes out. Some of these neighborhoods are ones that, as we saw earlier, reacted with considerable hostility when the first Negroes moved in. Indeed, these are the neighborhoods that are often the most explosive and produce some of the bitterest anti-Negro sentiment on the part of the whites.

The low integration attitudes of residents in substantially integrated neighborhoods are, however, more difficult to explain and suggest a considerable discrepancy between behavior and attitude. These are neighborhoods that are still attracting considerable numbers of white residents, and there is every reason to believe that most of them will continue to be integrated over the next five years and possibly beyond. Why then should there be the lowest support for equal rights for Negroes among residents of these neighborhoods? To a considerable extent, the answer to this question lies in the regional and socioeconomic characteristics of these neighborhoods, a significant portion of which are in the South where attitudes are traditionally more anti-integration. Also, as we have noted many times before, these neighborhoods are of lower socio-economic status.

Variations in Attitudes by Region and Socio-economic Status

There is and has always been a striking difference in attitudes toward Negroes between whites in the South and those living elsewhere. Because the regional differences are so marked, and the number of southern residents in our sample is so small, we shall have to limit the remainder of our analysis of white attitudes to those residents in our sample who are living outside the South.

On the question of pro-integration sentiment, open and moderately integrated neighborhoods remain the most positive, followed by the white segregated neighborhoods, the Negro segregated neighborhoods, and finally the substantially integrated neighborhoods. The socio-economic status of neighborhoods may also account for differences in integration attitudes. For example, greater education has been shown in many studies to be directly connected with positive attitudes toward Negroes. Substantially integrated and Negro segregated neighborhoods have a lower average education level than the other neighborhoods. It is quite likely that much of the remaining difference among the neighborhoods is due to differences in socio-economic status.

Small attitudinal differences persist among residents of different neighborhoods who have a high school education or less. Such persistence is noteworthy because there are substantial differences in attitudes according to the type of neighborhood these people live in. Among those with a high school education or less who live in white segregated, open, or moderately integrated neighborhoods, those living in open and moderately integrated neighborhoods are more favorable toward integration than those living in white segregated neighborhoods. It is, of course, not clear whether these differences reflect small changes in attitude that come from living in integrated neighborhoods, or whether the people who chose to live in integrated neighborhoods were favorably disposed to integration to begin with.

Conversely, at almost all levels of education, whites living in substantially integrated and Negro segregated neighborhoods look less favorably on integration than do residents of other types of neighborhoods. Here, too, it is difficult to tell if low integration attitudes derive from living in the neighborhood or were held before Negroes moved in, but the attitudes are clearly at variance with behavior.

It seems reasonable to conclude from these facts that behavior, at least as far as residential choice is concerned, is relatively independent of attitudes. However, several important points should be kept in mind. First, housing choices are constrained by many factors other than racial attitudes, notably economic considerations, a family's housing requirements, and the proximity of one's neighborhood to one's place of employment. Previous studies have shown that such factors are of overwhelming importance in determining housing choice. Whatever one's preference for integrated or segregated living, it is secondary to the more important question of where one can get the best apartment or house within one's financial means. It is hardly surprising, then, that attitudes toward integration are not of primary importance in deciding where to live.

Second, we have so far been considering general attitudes toward integration. Of particular interest in residential choice are attitudes toward equality of housing opportunities. Thus, we may find some interesting differences if we turn our attention to a single item—the right of whites to keep Negroes out of their neighborhoods.

Influence of Urbanization and Home Ownership on Housing Segregation Attitudes

Since World War II there has been an increasing movement of people from rural parts of the country to the larger metropolitan areas and, at least on the part of whites, a further movement out to the suburbs. This being the case, it is necessary to consider the extent to which living in central cities as opposed to living in suburbs is related to attitudes on housing integration. Our research shows, however, that none of these factors has any consistent or significant effect upon the attitudes toward integration of either city or suburban dwellers. For example, although white suburban residents tend to feel more strongly about their right to keep Negroes out of their neighborhoods than whites in central cities, the differences for the most part are small. The situation is reversed in substantially integrated areas, where white residents living in the central city are more likely to support the right to segregated living than suburbanites. The largest single difference between residents of central cities and of suburbs occurs among whites living in Negro segregated neighborhoods. Whites who live in suburban areas that are becoming Negro segregated are the most likely to agree that they have the right to prevent Negroes from moving into their neighborhoods. They, however, make up a very small group, and their situation is somewhat unusual.

There has been considerable speculation about the connection between home ownership and resistance to housing integration. Earlier we demonstrated that rental areas are somewhat more easily integrated. From this we speculated that an increase in the availability of rental units might remove one barrier to further integration of the suburbs. Although rental areas may be easier to integrate, a problem arises in that it is difficult to prevent them from becoming Negro segregated if there is significant imbalance favoring Negroes in the competition for housing. Our findings are not altogether clear, but it does appear that, on the whole, homeowners are slightly more inclined to believe in the right of whites to keep Negroes out of their neighborhoods. Curiously, among white residents in substantially integrated neighborhoods, it is the renters who are more likely to believe in white people's right to keep Negroes out. This reversal of attitudes between homeowners and renters may be indicative of the lesser involvement that renters characteristically have in their neighborhoods and the fact that they are somewhat more likely to react more quickly to changes, or even anticipated changes, in the neighborhood. It might also be due to the fact that homeowners are more likely to live in the suburbs, which tend to be characterized by less favorable attitudes toward integration. Unfortunately, neither of these two explanations can be sufficiently documented. Overall, then, urbanization and home ownership status or rental status do not show any strong or consistent connection with attitudes on housing integration.

Housing Market Variables

There is a considerable body of folk wisdom suggesting that one prime determinant of people's attitudes and behavior toward housing and integration is their past experience with, and expectation of, changes in the housing market. As one of our informants put it:

> No matter how liberal you think people are, no matter what pledge cards they sign or organizations they join, a funny thing comes over them when they hear that the first Negro family is going to move into their neighborhood. Some of them get scared. In this case not of the color of their skins—we've had every shade of skin in our pool for years and years. Plenty of all races, parties around here. It's their investment, their equity. They see themselves robbed of a valuable piece of property.

In spite of the fact that systematic studies have shown that racial integration does not, in and of itself, affect property values, this view is widespread and appears to affect people's behavior significantly.

That there is no evidence of a direct relation between racial integration and a decrease in property values does not preclude the possibility that in some instances integration may in fact be accompanied by—or, more likely, preceded by—a decline in property values. This can come about either through the aging of a neighborhood or because of some important change in the traditional demand for housing in a neighborhood. Thus, it is likely that the actions that whites take in the attempt to keep their neighborhood segregated may in fact decrease the demand for housing among other whites in the area— indeed, such actions may even precipitate the very decline in housing values that the actions were initially designed to forestall. Such actions are, of course, a classic example of the self-fulfilling prophecy.

In our interviews with neighborhood informants, we secured data on the changes in the demand for housing that can be used to assess the relation between changes in housing market variables and attitudes toward housing integration. In the three types of integrated neighborhoods, changes in property values and difficulty in selling houses have a definite and consistent relation to residents' attitudes toward racial integration. In those areas where there has been a drop in property values, or where it is more difficult to sell houses than it was five years ago, white residents are likely to assert that they have the right to keep their neighborhood segregated. The direction of cause and effect is difficult to determine. It is possible that in some neighborhoods negative attitudes toward integration do not merely precede the drop in property values but may be one of the factors causing the drop. For example, if many residents in a white segregated neighborhood who have strong anti-integration attitudes put their homes up for sale simultaneously when the first Negroes move in, prices are likely to drop sharply, particularly if the owners try to sell only to whites, who may be reluctant to buy in a neighborhood where panic appears to have set in. But, when housing prices drop for reasons unrelated to integration, the purchase of homes by Negroes able to afford the lower prices may cause whites to associate the drop in value with the increase in Negro buyers. If the greater demand for housing that results from opening up the neighborhood to a new market then causes the values to rise, there may be a decline (or at least no appreciable increase) in anti-integration sentiment.

For rental property, however, the picture is somewhat different. Only in substantially integrated neighborhoods are there significant differences in attitude toward housing integration, and these differences depend upon whether the demand for rental properties has improved or declined. Those white renters in neighborhoods where there are a large number of unoccupied apartments are apprehensive about the possibility that these vacancies will be filled by Negroes. White renters, in their fear, generally react by asserting strong anti-Negro sentiment. It is likely that these renters are concentrated in areas which probably will eventually become Negro segregated unless significant changes in the housing market occur. Our neighborhood informants, though, expect these areas to be stably integrated over the next five years.

In the white segregated areas, where there are more vacancies in rental properties, there is also a tendency to support housing segregation. It may be that whites in these areas are beginning to be apprehensive about segregation barriers being dropped in the face of the declining rental market among whites. As we saw earlier, the way in which a neighborhood reacted when the first Negroes moved in may well determine whether it will eventually become stably integrated or become Negro segregated.

These comparisons lead to the conclusion that among white residents in integrated neighborhoods, even in those that have very few Negroes, attitudes toward racial integration are strongly related to experiences with stability or change in the housing market over the past few years. While residents of open and moderately integrated neighborhoods are sensitive primarily to changes in the market for houses, residents of substantially integrated neighborhoods are sensitive to changes in both the sales and the rental markets. Indeed, when changes in the housing market are taken into consideration, the fairly consistent tendency for residents of substantially integrated neighborhoods to be more against racial integration is explained. In white segregated neighborhoods, however, housing market changes bear relatively little relation to attitudes toward racial segregation.

By and large, residents are more concerned with changes in the housing market and its economic impact than with the racial composition of the neighborhood. The attitudes of residents in neighborhoods that expect a large Negro increase and those in neighborhoods that do not are in fact relatively similar. Again, the most direct connection between housing values and racial attitudes is to be found in substantially integrated neighborhoods. These areas are much more likely to be near all-Negro or heavily Negro areas. Many of them, but by no means all, will have considerable Negro demand for housing that may substantially change their racial balance.

Although the informants' expectations of change in the proportion of Negroes and the potential Negro demand for housing did not reveal strong relations with residents' attitudes toward housing integration, residents' apprehensions about change do show a direct connection with anti-Negro attitudes. In those neighborhoods where residents say that their neighbors are very concerned about the neighborhood changing, a stronger segregationist spirit is usually found, regardless of the current level of integration in the neighborhood. In integrated neighborhoods residents' apprehensions about what is going to happen, whether or not they are reinforced by reality, are significant. Here, too, the important factor is the anticipation of potential economic loss rather than of an increase in Negro neighbors *per se*.

ATTITUDES OF NEGRO RESIDENTS

At the time this study was planned, integration was the generally accepted goal of almost all civil rights groups. We, therefore, limited our research on Negroes to an inves-

tigation of their attitudes toward the civil rights movement, in particular the movement's activities and their
own participation in them. (In retrospect, it is unfortunate
that we did not ask Negro respondents directly about their
views concerning the desirability of integrated living.
Since the completion of this study, there has been a growth
in a black nationalist ideology that may have brought
about radical changes in the attitudes of black residents.)

We found (Table 8.2) that attitudes toward civil rights
issues were relatively alike in all the neighborhood types
with one striking exception. A higher proportion of Negro

Table 8.2 *Selected Attitudes and Behavior Related to Civil Rights,
by Neighborhood Type (Percent of Negro Residents Agreeing or
Disagreeing as Indicated)*

| Item | Neighborhood Type | | | |
	Open	Moder-ately Inte-grated	Sub-stan-tially Inte-grated	Negro Segre-gated
Most white people would really like Negroes to have their rights (Agree)	60	70	62	47
The federal government would do very little about civil rights if it weren't for demonstrations (Disagree)	30	30	34	27
Sometimes I think Negroes should not have supported some of the civil rights demonstrations I have read about (Agree)	63	75	76	63
Riots like the one in Watts help the Negro cause as much as they hurt it (Disagree)	58	62	60	55
Attended civil rights rally (Yes)	49	19	16	15
Participated in civil rights demonstration (Yes)	20	10	7	9
N	(69)	(49)	(455)	(243)

residents of open neighborhoods have attended civil rights rallies or participated in civil rights demonstrations than residents of the other neighborhoods. While the low proportion of Negro residents in substantially integrated and Negro segregated neighborhoods who have attended civil rights rallies is partially due to the fact that many of these neighborhoods are in the South—where participation in civil rights demonstrations and attendance at civil rights rallies is negligible—eliminating the southern neighborhoods only brings the proportion up to the level of the non-southern moderately integrated neighborhoods and does not come up to the level achieved by Negro residents of open neighborhoods. It would appear, therefore, that there is a significant difference in the degree of participation in civil rights activities between Negro residents of open neighborhoods and those in other types of integrated neighborhoods.

This difference can be understood in greater detail by looking at the connection between level of education and attendance at civil rights rallies for residents of each of the various neighborhood types. As we saw in Table 5.2, Negro residents of open neighborhoods have considerably more education than Negroes in other areas. This leads to the hypothesis that there is a relation between education and attendance at civil rights rallies. When we control for education (Table 8.3), we do in fact find that there is a strong connection between attendance at civil rights rallies and one's level of education.

The fact that neighborhood differences appear to persist even after controlling for education suggests that the Negroes in open neighborhoods may be "pioneers"— which is to say, the first few Negroes to move into a previously all-white neighborhood. To be the first Negro to move into an all-white neighborhood requires a commitment to integration and, given the frequently rough response on the part of white residents, courage of a kind that is wholly consistent with participation in the civil rights movement.

Table 8.3 *Attendance at Civil Rights Rally and Neighborhood Type, by Education (Percent of Negro Residents Attending Civil Rights Rallies)*

Education	Open	Moder- ately Inte- grated	Sub- stan- tially Inte- grated	Negro Segre- grated
		Neighborhood Type		
Part high school or less	*ᵃ(10)	8 (24)	9 (301)	9 (153)
High school	* (11)	* (8)	21 (94)	14 (56)
More than high school	60 (48)	* (13)	41 (66)	34 (41)

ᵃ Asterisks indicate too few cases for reliable percentaging.

It may be surprising that Negroes with higher education are more likely to have participated in civil rights rallies. The relationship, however, shows up consistently in all neighborhoods. There is, indeed, good reason to believe that the more highly educated are in general more suspicious of the goodwill of whites and are considerably more militant in their attitudes. An exception is the general feeling among Negroes that riots would do some good, an item on which there are no differences among educational groups.

SUMMARY AND DISCUSSION

The findings in this chapter indicate that variations in whites' attitudes toward integration are associated with two variables, region of residence and education, which do not directly reflect the integrated status of the neighborhood in which the individuals live. Thus, it would appear that cultural and personal variables play a major role in affecting one's overall attitudes on racial integration, and that these attitudes may in fact be at variance with one's actual behavior. Insofar as neighborhood variables are important above and beyond these cultural and personal matters, they show up most clearly when it comes to changes in the housing market that affect the economic stake an individual has in his residence, whether it be his equity or his rent. Such findings are consistent with the argument presented earlier in this chapter suggesting that general attitudes would have relatively little role in housing choice and that economic considerations are of greater importance. When people live where the housing market is stable with relatively little fluctuation or threat to their investments, more tolerance can be expected. When there is a threat to investment, however, less tolerance, indeed often open hostility, is more likely to prevail.

The findings in this chapter on Negro attitudes suggest that integrated living by itself will not produce positive attitudes toward whites. In some instances integration may lead not to positive improvement in race relations but to a reinforcement of the belief that whites are bigoted and anti-Negro.

Although changes in real estate market conditions are associated with white attitudes toward housing segregation, white residents who have had past experiences with living in integrated neighborhoods do in fact currently have more favorable attitudes toward integration than those who have not previously lived in integrated neighborhoods. While the data do not enable us to answer questions of cause and effect definitively, there is at least some suggestion that, on the average, a symmetry exists between the experiences of Negroes and whites in integrated neighborhoods. For the Negroes, the environment is frequently hostile and the white residents unfriendly. Whites, on the other hand, pay relatively little attention to Negro families. At best, there is some perception of the fact that they now have Negroes for neighbors and that the world of their neighborhood has not fallen apart.

Given the frequently negative experiences of Negroes in integrated neighborhoods, it is not surprising that housing integration *per se* has not been a high priority item on the agenda of equal rights groups or of Negro leaders. In a 1963 NORC national survey, only 1 percent of the Negro respondents put "no discrimination in housing" as the most important right to be worked for, and only 22 percent mentioned the "right to live in white neighborhoods" as a right wanted by almost all Negroes (see Schwartz, 1967). An unpublished 1967 NORC survey of Negroes living in the North and West indicated that almost two-thirds of all Negroes preferred to live in neighborhoods that were mostly or totally Negro, *regardless of whether or not they currently lived in integrated neighborhoods.* A study by Campbell and Schuman (1968) of racial attitudes in fifteen cities showed that while 1 percent of the Negro respondents reported wanting to live in mostly white neighborhoods, 85 percent reported either that they preferred neighborhoods in which the racial percentage was about 50–50, or that the racial composition of the neighborhood made no difference to them.

A reasonable inference to be drawn from these data is that Negroes, like whites, are concerned more with the adequacy of the housing than with the racial composition of the neighborhood. No more than whites do Negroes want to be a minority in their neighborhood, and they prefer, other things being equal, to live in areas where they are a majority group, or at least in a neighborhood where there is no clear majority group. If other things are not equal and better housing is available only in areas that are predominately white, there will be some Negro demand for housing in predominately white areas. However, if good quality housing were to become available near predominately Negro areas, it is evident that such housing would be in much higher demand by Negroes. This fact makes it unlikely that predominately white neighborhoods near predominately Negro areas will remain stably integrated over a long period. Only if there is some substantial change in the reaction of white residents to Negro families that move into predominately white neighborhoods can much change in this pattern be expected.

9 *Integration in the Schools*

THE INTIMATE relationship between housing segregation and school segregation has often been noted by those concerned with racial integration in the public schools. Because most public schools enroll students from the surrounding areas, racial segregation of neighborhoods usually will result in racial segregation of schools even if the local school boards do not take deliberate steps to maintain segregation. The influence of the racial composition of schools on housing decisions has been studied somewhat less, although there is widespread belief that changing the racial composition of schools plays an important role in accelerating racial change in transitional neighborhoods. Stabilizing the racial balance in schools is seen by some as an effective device to prevent a substantially integrated neighborhood from becoming a changing or Negro segregated neighborhood. Our conviction that there was a close connection between housing integration and school integration led us to focus considerable attention on the role of schools in neighborhood life.

In this chapter we explore both the extent of racial integration in the schools attended by the children living in the neighborhoods under study and the attitudes of the residents of these neighborhoods toward their schools. We use data both from the neighborhood informants and from the residents' sample. As a reminder, our segregated control neighborhoods are not a random sample of all non-integrated neighborhoods but are matched as nearly as possible with our integrated neighborhoods on the basis of socio-economic status and location within the metropolitan area. Thus, these results cannot be generalized to give any overall estimates of the degree of segregation in the schools in the United States.

RACIAL COMPOSITION OF SCHOOLS

Our findings show that even in white segregated neighborhoods, on the average, 50 percent of the schools are attended by both Negro and white students (Table 9.1). There are also some all-Negro schools in these neighborhoods. The presence of all-Negro schools is explained by the fact that white segregated neighborhoods sometimes contain, or are adjacent to, pockets of all-Negro areas with housing that is not of comparable value to the housing occupied by the whites. By our definition, therefore, these

Table 9.1 *Racial Composition of School by Neighborhood Type (Percent of Schools: Data from Informants)*

| | | | | Neighborhood Type | | |
| | | | | | Substantially Integrated | |
Racial Composition of School	White Segregated	Open	Moderately Integrated	North and West	South	Negro Segregated
Both Negro and white students	50	73	88	93	60	69
All white	48	27	12	6	12	5
All Negro.	2	0	0	1	28	26
Total	100	100	100	100	100	100

neighborhoods did not qualify as integrated.

An examination of the three types of integrated neighborhoods reveals a pattern more in line with ordinary expectations. As one goes from open to moderately integrated to substantially integrated neighborhoods (in the North and West, at least—that is, from neighborhoods with a very small proportion of Negro residents to those with a larger proportion—the average percentage of schools attended by both Negroes and whites increases and the number of all-white schools decreases.

In the Negro segregated neighborhoods (which also include some changing neighborhoods that are still largely white), we find a substantial proportion of integrated schools, as well as some all-white schools.[1] Furthermore, in these neighborhoods the proportion of all-Negro schools is considerably higher than in any other type of neighborhood, except for the substantially integrated neighborhoods in the South. As time goes on, of course, we expect that the all-white schools will disappear and the proportion of integrated schools will decrease, unless some action stabilizes changing neighborhoods or there is a radical realignment of school boundaries or a busing plan.

Another measure of the degree of school integration in our neighborhoods is the proportion of parents of school-age children in each of the types of neighborhood who have children in integrated schools. We asked each resident in our sample who had children in school a series of questions about each of the schools attended by his children. (Our conclusions are based on responses to the first school mentioned by respondents, although some had children in two and occasionally three different schools.) Included in these questions was "Do both white and Negro children attend (*name of school*)?" And, if the answer was yes, "Approximately what percentage of the children at (*name of school*) are Negro, would you guess?"

A majority of the respondents with children who live in

[1]These schools are in fact all in southern nonurban areas.

the white segregated neighborhoods have at least one child in a school attended by both Negroes and whites. Our findings accord with those of previous studies of racial segregation in schools. In general, the proportion of white parents with children in all-white schools declines as a neighborhood's proportion of Negro residents increases. The white residents in Negro segregated neighborhoods who have children in all-white schools live in rural areas in the South.

For the most part, the pattern of school integration by neighborhood type is consistent, allowing for such variables as region, size of place, urbanization, public versus private or parochial schools, and elementary versus high schools. For whites living in integrated neighborhoods, the size of place has little bearing on the likelihood of their children attending integrated schools; for Negroes, the probability of their children attending integrated schools is higher in the larger cities. For whites in white segregated neighborhoods the pattern reverses, with those living in the larger metropolitan areas being less likely to have their children attending integrated schools than those in smaller and nonmetropolitan areas. This difference may be due to the greater number of suburbs in the larger metropolitan areas, since whites living in segregated suburbs are much less likely to have children in integrated schools.

In almost all types of neighborhoods, public schools are more likely to be integrated than private or parochial schools, and high schools are more likely to be integrated than elementary schools. The major exception is that Negroes in both substantially integrated and Negro segregated neighborhoods are more likely to have their children attend an integrated school at the elementary level than at the high school level.

The reports of the residents indicate that there is a neighborhood pattern in the percentage of Negroes in the schools that is similar to the pattern in the percentage of schools attended by both Negro and white students (Table 9.2). It is difficult to know whether to be optimistic or pes-

Table 9.2 Percentage of Negroes in First School Listed, by Neighborhood Types (Percent of Parents with Children Attending School)

	White Parents						Negro Parents	
	Neighborhood Type						Neighborhood Type	
				Substantially Integrated				
Percent Negro in School	White Segregated	Open	Moderately Integrated	North and West	South	Negro Segregated	Substantially Integrated	Negro Segregated
0	41	24	13	9	10	15	0	0
1-4	30	52	32	15	41	27	1	1
5-19	13	17	31	13	35	27	4	5
20-49	14	7	18	35	10	15	12	12
50 or more	2	0	6	28	4	15	83	82
Total	100	100	100	100	100	99[a]	100	100
N	(206)	(343)	(235)	(57)	(74)	(26)	(212)	(124)

[a] Not 100 percent because of rounding.

simistic about these figures. On the optimistic side, it is clear that there are many white parents who are sending their children to schools that contain substantial proportions of Negro students—this is true even for residents of white segregated neighborhoods. On the pessimistic side, even in the substantially integrated neighborhoods, a very high proportion of Negro parents have children in schools in which Negroes are the majority. This fact indicates that neighborhoods that are, by our definition, stably integrated still have school systems which are almost completely segregated. In thinking about what this may mean, it should be remembered that most of the substantially integrated neighborhoods contain only 10 to 20 percent Negro residents, so the schools are not reflecting the overall proportions in the neighborhood. A substantial proportion (31 percent) of the Negro students in schools that are 50 percent or more Negro are, in fact, in all-Negro schools.

The data on integration in the schools parallel in many ways the data on integration in the neighborhoods. We found a surprisingly large number of schools attended by both Negro and white students, just as we found a surprisingly large number of neighborhoods into which both Negroes and whites were moving. When we look further, however, we see that the proportion of Negroes in the integrated schools is typically very small, just as the proportion of Negroes in the integrated neighborhoods is typically very small. While these data suggest that in a large number of areas we have moved beyond token integration, we still have not reached a state in which there is genuine freedom of residence.

SCHOOL ATTENDANCE PATTERNS

So far we have considered only the degree of integration in neighborhood schools. In some instances, particularly in neighborhoods that are changing to Negro segregated, there may be some local adjustments that allow white parents to continue sending their children to white segregated schools, such as private schools or public schools in some other neighborhood. The latter is sometimes difficult because of neighborhood school attendance requirements in public schools. There are, however, frequently ways around these requirements for white parents if they are willing to pay for transportation.

There are relatively few differences in attendance patterns among our neighborhoods; perhaps the most notable differences occur in the substantially integrated and Negro segregated neighborhoods. In the Negro segregated areas, white parents of elementary school children are more likely than white parents in other neighborhoods to send their children to schools outside the neighborhood—either to public schools or to private or parochial schools. As noted in the previous section, there were white parents in southern neighborhoods that we classified as Negro segregated who in fact had children in all-white schools. The fact that a higher proportion of residents in these southern neighborhoods say that the school attended by their children is outside the neighborhood probably reflects the rural character of many of the neighborhoods rather than a deliberate adjustment of attendance patterns in response to school integration. At the high school level, there do not appear to be any significant differences in attendance patterns among our different neighborhoods.

It appears, then, that adjustments in attendance patterns either by the use of private or parochial schools or by sending children outside the neighborhood exist as a possible response to the changing racial patterns of the schools. There is not a significant number of white parents with elementary school children who exercise this option. Thus, while differing attendance patterns may be of particular relevance in some changing neighborhoods, this is not a very widespread phenomenon or one that is significant in maintaining a stably integrated neighborhood.

QUALITY OF SCHOOLS

Since we believed that schools play an important role in

attracting or keeping residents in the neighborhood, we were particularly concerned with the opinions held by our neighborhood informants and by the parents of school-age children about the quality of the schools in their neighborhoods. Thus, for each of the schools mentioned by our informants or by the parents, we asked a series of questions about the quality of the school, particularly about attendance or the degree of overcrowding, the physical condition of the school, the educational program, and its extracurricular activities. We also asked the parents for an overall rating. Except for ratings on crowding, there is a tendency for informants and parents in both the southern substantially integrated and the Negro segregated areas to give schools lower ratings. As noted earlier, however, both these types of neighborhoods have substantially lower income levels than other neighborhoods. When the median income of the neighborhood is controlled, the differences among neighborhood types are considerably reduced. Among poorer neighborhoods, however, schools in the Negro segregated neighborhoods still receive generally lower ratings. The differences between rich and poor neighborhoods far outweigh the differences among types of neighborhoods.

One sharp difference is the contrast between the ratings of schools given by Negro parents and those given by white parents in both substantially integrated neighborhoods outside the South and Negro segregated neighborhoods. Negroes in both substantially integrated and Negro segregated neighborhoods and whites in southern substantially integrated neighborhoods are considerably more critical of the schools and give them substantially lower ratings than do whites in Negro segregated or non-southern substantially integrated neighborhoods. This tendency for Negro respondents to give poorer ratings is not restricted to schools, but reflects a more general tendency to give poorer ratings than whites to all public and private facilities in their neighborhoods. While we do not have data that explain these differences definitively, it seems quite likely that they reflect the realities of life for Negroes in America today, and perhaps also for some white southerners.

Some indirect evidence that these varying opinions have a basis in reality is found in the differences in school ratings given by both Negro and white parents to schools with differing proportions of Negro students. If it is true, as frequently charged by both white and Negro parents, that the quality of schooling declines as the proportion of Negro students increases, the difference between Negro and white residents' ratings should disappear when we control for the percentage of Negroes in the school. When the distinction by neighborhood type is dropped and schools are rated by the percentage of Negro students, the ratings of the schools on educational programs and the overall ratings become lower as the proportion of Negroes begins to exceed 20 percent and drop off sharply when the schools become predominantly Negro. On these two variables both Negro and white parents rate schools at approximately the same levels when the student body is composed of from 20 to 49 percent Negro, and both white and Negro parents give the majority-Negro schools much poorer ratings. The fact that Negro residents whose children are in majority-Negro schools rate them even lower on educational programs and overall ratings than do white residents whose children are in majority-Negro schools probably reflects the fact that a substantial proportion of the Negro parents have children attending all-Negro schools, whereas most of the small number of white parents with children in majority-Negro schools have them in schools that are nearer to 50–50.

THE ROLE OF SCHOOLS IN MAINTAINING THE
STABILITY OF THE NEIGHBORHOOD

The quality of public schools in a neighborhood is often cited by real estate agents as an important factor in attracting residents to a particular neighborhood. While schools are of particular importance to the 50 percent of those families who have children of school age, they also have some effect on families who do not have children currently in school. For example, the quality of neighborhood schools may be important for young couples who are either just beginning their families or who have preschool children and who will be making housing decisions in the relatively near future. It is even true to some extent for families with no children or with children who are grown, because the general quality of the schools is one indicator, although for their purposes a relatively less important one, of the general quality of life in the community.

The importance of schools for housing choice should not be overestimated. While we acknowledge that schools play a role in attracting residents to a community, our knowledge about the most important factors influencing housing decisions would not lead us to expect schools to be an overwhelmingly important attraction for most families. For some families, schools may be a critical negative factor if they are, in fact, below the acceptable limits of quality. In short, the role of schools in the life of a community is complex, and dramatic differences among our neighborhoods should not be expected in either informants' or residents' evaluations of the importance of neighborhood schools.

One way we approached the problem of measuring the impact of schools on the neighborhood was to ask our informants, "In general would you say that this school is a positive attraction, has very little effect, or has a negative effect in bringing people into the neighborhood and keeping them from moving?" The ratings we got are in line with the ratings of school quality that we discussed previously. Schools are most likely to be seen as a positive attraction in the white segregated neighborhoods. In the open and moderately integrated neighborhoods, a majority of the schools are seen as a positive factor, although the proportion is somewhat smaller than in the white segregated neighborhoods. In the substantially integrated and Negro segregated neighborhoods, the proportions drop below 50 percent, which corresponds with the generally lower ratings in school quality given by the informants in these neighborhoods. Although schools are less of a positive factor in substantially integrated and Negro segregated neighborhoods, among all neighborhood types there are very few neighborhoods in which schools are seen as a negative factor. As viewed by informants, schools either play a positive role in attracting residents or, at worst, have no effect—in only a few exceptional cases do they really have a negative effect.

While these overall ratings are of some interest, they reveal relatively little about the relation between school integration and the role of the schools in maintaining the stability of the neighborhood. As has been shown, a large proportion of white parents send their children to schools that are integrated, but the proportion of white students in schools that are more than 20 percent Negro is very small. While there are some spectacular cases of parents boycotting schools and harassing school boards over boundary changes, our data indicate clearly that there is considerable willingness on the part of white parents, regardless of their attitudes toward integration, to send their children to integrated schools when the proportion of Negro students is relatively small. Although one may speculate about what constitutes a "small" percentage, it seems clear that the willingness of white parents to send their children to integrated schools goes down as the proportion of Negroes in those schools increases.

What the "tipping point" might be is a subject of considerable speculation. We expect that there is no absolute answer to the question of how small is "small," and that the definition of "small" will vary with the past experiences of people in the neighborhood and the residents' expectations about the future racial composition of their own neighborhood and of surrounding neighborhoods using the same schools. One way to explore indirectly the relation between the current situation and expectations of future change is to look at the kind of neighborhood in conjunction with the percentage of Negroes that live in adjacent neighborhoods but share schools with our neighborhoods. In spite of the prevalence of a neighborhood school policy, school boundaries are not exactly coterminous with the residents' sense of neighborhood boundaries, and children from adjacent neighborhoods frequently attend school together. Thus, we would expect that the proportion of Negroes in adjacent neighborhoods using the same schools would be of importance in assessing the role of schools in maintaining the stability of the neighborhood.

In order to test this notion, we obtained data on the proportion of Negroes in adjacent neighborhoods from which children attended the same schools as children in our neighborhoods. For each of our neighborhoods we constructed a measure of the maximum percentage of Negroes living in adjacent neighborhoods who shared schools with it—that is, the largest proportion of Negroes in any of the adjacent neighborhoods that shared at least some public school facilities with our neighborhood. The differences among neighborhood types are considerably reduced for all neighborhoods whose maximum percentage of Negroes in adjacent neighborhoods is less than 20 percent. In all types of neighborhoods that are adjacent to neighborhoods in which the maximum percentage of Negroes is 20 percent or greater, schools are less likely to be rated as a positive attraction. Schools are least likely to be noted as a positive factor in substantially integrated neighborhoods adjacent to the more heavily populated Negro areas.

The one type of neighborhood in which schools may play a really significant role in its future stability is the substantially integrated neighborhood that is adjacent to at least one neighborhood with a high proportion of Negroes. At present these neighborhoods meet our criteria for stable integration—that is, both Negroes and whites are currently moving into housing of comparable value and our informants expect that this situation will continue for at least the next five years. In the long run, however, it is likely that many of these neighborhoods will eventually change and become all Negro. The fact that the schools in these neighborhoods are much less likely to be rated as a positive feature of the neighborhood suggests that signs of trouble are already appearing, and that schools are thought to be (and may actually be) declining in quality or are changing in their proportion of Negroes at a much faster rate than the neighborhood itself. It is likely that these are the types of neighborhoods in which ameliorative action by school officials could prevent a change from the substantially integrated to the Negro segregated category. Such action would require taking steps to improve or maintain the quality of the school and/or to limit the proportion of Negro students in the school, probably through quotas or a busing arrangement. While these remedies are usually not very palatable to school officials, our data suggest that this is the one type of neighborhood that might well benefit from imaginative and bold action to make the schools attractive to residents of the community.

CONCERN OVER PROPORTION OF NEGROES IN SCHOOLS

We suggested earlier that the perception of the level of integration that might provide a "tipping point" would vary depending on the circumstances in which people found themselves. We obtained data from our residents' questionnaire that would help us illuminate the dynamics of this situation somewhat more fully. We asked each resident who had a child in school to tell us not only the percentage of Negro students in the school but also, "Would you be concerned if the proportion of Negro children in (*name of school*) rose beyond a certain percentage?" And, if the answer was yes, "What percentage would that be?" We were thus able to investigate differences across neighborhoods as well as among individuals who have children in schools with differing percentages of Negroes.

There are a few differences among neighborhood types, but these are relatively small. The most notable difference is the larger percentage of white parents in white segregated neighborhoods and, not surprisingly, in substantially integrated neighborhoods in the South who would be concerned if even a small percentage of Negroes were in the schools. Again it becomes apparent that southern attitudes are markedly different and that white parents in the South would be extremely unhappy if the schools became integrated, even if the proportion of Negroes were small.

Perhaps the most surprising response came from the large percentage of white parents who said that they would not be concerned regardless of an increase in the proportion of Negro children in the schools beyond any particular percentage. Given the current experiences and expectations of the majority of white respondents in our survey, we interpret these results to mean that most white parents are not concerned about the proportion of Negroes in the schools their children attend *within the range of proportions that they reasonably expect will occur in their neighborhoods.* Thus, if many respondents do not see the possibility of the proportion of Negroes in the schools in their neighborhoods rising above, say, 25 percent, and anything within this range is tolerable to them, they would not express a particular concern about the percentage of Negroes. Such an interpretation suggests that many white respondents have difficulty even considering the possibility that they might live in areas where the proportion of Negroes would become large enough to exceed the limits of toleration that they have set for themselves.

Partial support for this interpretation is found when we control for the maximum percentage of Negroes in adjacent neighborhoods that share schools with our neighborhoods. The proportion of parents "not concerned" is lower in those moderately integrated neighborhoods where the maximum percentage of Negroes in adjacent neighborhoods that share schools is greater than 20 percent. For residents of these neighborhoods that currently have few Negro residents, schools with substantial Negro enrollment are a possibility, even if not currently a reality, and their lack of concern drops away. Such is not the case, however, for residents of open neighborhoods, where the lack of concern among parents in neighborhoods adjacent to ones with a maximum percentage of Negroes of 20 or greater is comparable to that of parents in moderately integrated neighborhoods adjacent to ones with less than 20 percent Negroes. The small number of cases in the former group, however, suggests that the high proportion of "not concerned" parents may be due to special circumstances in one or two neighborhoods. Also, the percentage of Negroes in adjacent areas does not affect dramatically the parents in the substantially integrated neighborhoods.

It should be remembered that there are some white parents, although not very many, who are currently sending their children to schools in which the proportion of Negroes is already 50 percent or greater. If we look at current school experience and the percentage of Negroes that would cause concern, we see a correlation between one's current actions and the level at which one would be concerned. The higher the current percentage of Negroes in schools attended by white respondents' children, the higher the percentage of Negroes the respondent is likely to mention as causing concern. While the vast majority of those who indicate concern are still doing so at 50 percent or less, there is a small proportion of white parents who say that they would not be concerned until their children were in a substantial minority position.

It appears that there may be a shifting level of tolerance for levels of integration that reflects the circumstances in which people live. White residents, with some notable exceptions, are willing to accept some level of school integration so long as the proportion of Negroes in the schools is relatively small. The definition of "small" varies somewhat, although on the whole it appears to be in the range of up to 25 percent. This is not a fixed point, and as one's experience with particular schools varies, higher levels of acceptance may well result.

SUMMARY

In this chapter we have examined several aspects of school integration and their relation to housing integration. In general, we found that there is a positive relation between the proportion of Negro residents in the neighborhood and the proportion of families with children in schools attended by both Negro and white children. In many ways the data on schools reflect our general findings on neighborhood integration. We found a surprisingly large number of schools attended by both Negro and white students, even in neighborhoods that are all white; we also found that the proportion of Negroes in the integrated schools is typically very small, as is the proportion of Negro families in the integrated neighborhoods.

There are few differences in attendance patterns among the neighborhood types. Although the possibility of adjustments in attendance patterns is frequently discussed among those who have worked in areas of substantial racial integration, we found no evidence that any significant number of white parents are shifting schools for their children in response to the racial composition of the neighborhood.

Our data show that there is little difference in the quality of schools among white segregated, open, and moderately integrated neighborhoods, but schools in many of the southern substantially integrated and the Negro segregated neighborhoods are judged to be inferior to those in the other types of neighborhoods. We interpret these differences to be primarily a function of the differing income levels in the substantially integrated and Negro segregated neighborhoods. Although it is also true that the ratings of schools tend to decline as the proportion of Negro students increases, we feel that this difference primarily reflects the income differential between Negroes and whites. This difference is so great that schools with large proportions of Negro students almost invariably are schools with large proportions of children from families of low socio-economic status. That schools should be inferior for children from poor families is a tragic fact of our society—a fact indicating perhaps more clearly than any other reported in this study how the present patterns of inequality will be perpetuated for many years to come.

Investigation of the role of schools in maintaining the stability of the neighborhood indicates that schools play an important role only in a limited set of neighborhoods that have special characteristics. Although schools are rated as a positive feature more commonly in white segregated neighborhoods than in any others, the data indicate that schools may play a significant role in the future stability of the neighborhood only in those substantially integrated areas where there is high Negro demand for housing. In these neighborhoods, rapid changes in the proportion of Negro students in the schools or in the perceived quality of the schools may precipitate a decline in white demand for housing and upset the stability of the neighborhood.

Examination of the data from several points of view reveals no evidence that there is a fixed "tipping point" for white residents, but rather that there are differing tolerance levels that change as a function of experience. The existence of a dynamic level of concern suggests that change itself is not necessarily a threat to stable integration as long as it does not occur too rapidly.

10 *Churches in Integrated Neighborhoods*

IN THIS CHAPTER we first assess the extent of racial integration in the churches. Then, focusing only on those respondents who reported that both whites and Negroes attended their church, we investigate their attitudes toward integration in their church and the extent of interracial social contacts there.

EXTENT OF RACIAL INTEGRATION IN CHURCHES

Of all the respondents in our survey who said that members of their family attended a church or temple, 17 percent, or slightly more than one in six, reported that both races were represented in their congregation, with Negroes comprising 2 percent or more of the total membership. Among whites, another 25 percent attended churches that were virtually all white—that is, churches which Negroes attended but constituted 1 percent or less of the total membership.

The limited amount of racial integration in churches is underscored by the rather generous definition of an "interracial" congregation that was adopted in this chapter—

namely, one in which both races held membership and Negroes constituted 2 percent or more of the total. Had we defined as interracial only those congregations that had a Negro membership of at least 11 percent, then only 3 percent of the white households in our survey would have been classified as attending an interracial church. Of the approximately 2,300 white families reporting that they attended church, only one went to a church the majority of whose members were Negro. Finally, membership in an interracial church was greater among Catholics than among Protestants: 26 percent of the Catholic families interviewed attended an "interracial" church as compared to 9 percent of the Protestant families.

In the above data all our respondents have been lumped together regardless of the level of integration of the neighborhood they live in, or whether they live in integrated or segregated neighborhoods. Table 10.1 presents the percentage of white churchgoers reporting membership in an interracial church within each of the neighborhood types. The percentages increase with an increase in the proportion of Negroes in the neighborhood. Even in Negro segregated neighborhoods, however, 37 percent of the white churchgoers attended interracial churches, while the

Table 10.1 *Racial Composition of Churches Attended and Neighborhood Type, Among Whites*

	Neighborhood Type					
				Substantially Integrated		
	White Segregated	Open	Moderately Integrated	North and West	South	Negro Segregated
Percent of households attending "interracial" churches	8	15	20	40	7	37
N	(450)	(817)	(612)	(180)	(201)	(83)

balance attended churches that were 1 percent Negro or less. Were we to use a more stringent definition of an "interracial" church—one that required at least one-tenth of the congregation to be Negro—we would find that only 11 percent of the white residents of Negro segregated neighborhoods could claim membership in interracial churches.

More specifically, in attempting to discern an association between the level of neighborhood integration and the level of integration in the churches attended by the neighborhood residents, we are clearly assuming that the churches are located in the same neighborhoods as their members. This is, of course, not always the case. Protestants and Jews are free to choose from a variety of congregations without being limited geographically. This is less true among Catholics, but even here membership across parish boundaries does exist, especially among Catholics who do not have children in parochial elementary schools.

The data for white segregated neighborhoods are more difficult to interpret. Given the already low proportion of all white churchgoers who attend interracial churches, about 17 percent, it is difficult to explain why the proportion attending interracial churches *located within* their own all-white neighborhoods is as high as it is (12 percent). The Negroes who account for the integration in these churches undoubtedly come from adjacent neighborhoods. Our data reveal that Negroes constituted almost 6 percent of the population in all neighborhoods adjoining the white segregated control neighborhoods in this study.

There was at least *some* church integration in neighborhoods that were all white, as well as in those that were open and, to a greater extent, in those that were moderately integrated. Of whites who live in open and moderately integrated neighborhoods but travel to a church outside their neighborhood, about 20 percent attend interracial churches. Among whites living in segregated neighborhoods who attend a church outside their neighborhood, only 3 percent go to interracial churches. Indeed, it is those who travel outside their neighborhoods who lower the overall level of attendance at inter-racial churches among residents of white segregated neighborhoods.

We view the difference between whites in all-white and integrated neighborhoods in their attendance at a church outside the neighborhood as resulting from different reactions to the prospect of attending an interracial church in their own neighborhood. Those who live in all-white neighborhoods are less tolerant in their integration attitudes than those in open and moderately integrated neighborhoods, and consequently respond by traveling outside the neighborhood to a segregated church.

Comparing integrated neighborhoods surrounded by neighborhoods with relatively few Negroes (less than 10 percent, on the average) with those surrounded by relatively large numbers of Negroes (10 percent or more), the results are surprising. We had supposed that the more Negroes physically present in adjacent neighborhoods, the greater would be the proportion of biracial churches in our sample neighborhoods. This, as it turns out, is not the case. For example, in northern and western open neighborhoods with adjacent communities containing relatively few Negroes, 41 percent of the churches are attended by both races. In those neighborhoods which have adjacent communities with relatively large numbers of Negroes, only 23 percent of the churches are biracial. A similar difference exists among moderately integrated neighborhoods.

How do we explain the fact that where there are relatively large numbers of Negroes available in surrounding neighborhoods for membership in churches, fewer churches are attended by both races? We suspect that in those neighborhoods where the contiguous areas are more heavily Negro (10 percent or more), there is a greater likelihood that an all-Negro church is present nearby which the Negro residents can attend. On the other hand, where the surrounding areas contain relatively few Negroes (less than

10 percent), there are comparatively few all-Negro churches to attract the Negroes who reside in integrated neighborhoods. They are faced with the alternatives of traveling some distance to all-Negro churches or, as our data suggest, attending predominantly white churches in which they provide token integration.

The crucial factor is the availability of an all-Negro church. Where there are too few Negroes to organize and support such a church, they will be dispersed among the existing white churches.

Partial corroboration of this, at least for open neighborhoods, obtains when the location of the neighborhood is considered. In open suburban neighborhoods, many churches are attended by both races; in open central-city neighborhoods, relatively few are so integrated. Again, the paucity of all-Negro churches in the suburbs necessitates Negro attendance at the existing churches, resulting in at least token integration in two of every five churches.

ATTITUDES TOWARD CURRENT CHURCH INTEGRATION

What are the attitudes toward the church integration that does exist in the neighborhoods we surveyed? Those churchgoers who reported that their church was integrated were asked, "Are you pleased or unhappy that (*name of church*) has both white and Negro members?" Slightly less than half our respondents said that they were "pleased," about half said that they "didn't care," and only 2 percent said that they were "unhappy."

Table 10.2 presents the proportion of residents reporting church integration who said they were "pleased" that their church was attended by both whites and Negroes. The greater satisfaction with church integration among Negroes is immediately apparent; in each type of neighborhood for which we have sufficient data, the proportion of Negroes expressing satisfaction with church integration exceeds the proportion among whites by 20 percentage points or more. Among whites, the greatest tol-

Table 10.2 *Acceptance of Church Integration and Neighborhood Type, by Race (Percent "Pleased" Church Is Integrated)*

Race	White Segregated	Neighborhood Type			
		Open	Moderately Integrated	Substantially Integrated	Negro Segregated
White	39 (128)	50 (367)	44 (291)	33 (125)	31 (42)
Negro	–	*ª (3)	* (19)	69 (94)	51 (47)

ª Asterisks indicate too few cases for reliable percentaging.

erance for existing integration in the church (50 percent) is found in open neighborhoods, which are characterized by some, though not extensive, residential integration. These data are consistent with the finding that white residents of open neighborhoods have the highest pro-integration scores. Indeed, it is possible that the apparent acceptance of church integration in open neighborhoods has little to do with the churches themselves but is simply another manifestation of a generalized racial tolerance.

Turning to variables other than neighborhood type in considering attitudes toward church integration, we find, first, that Protestants are more likely than Catholics to report that they are "pleased" at the fact that their church is integrated, although Catholics are actually more likely than Protestants to attend interracial churches. This suggests that, for Catholics, behavior may come in advance of attitudes—in other words, the very strong tradition among Catholics of attending the local parish church may override any personal displeasure about the congregation's integrated status. For Protestants, the selection of a congregation is a more voluntary act; and those who have selected a church attended by Negroes, or who have decided to remain in their church after it has become integrated, have already exhibited comparatively tolerant behavior. It is, therefore, understandable that such Protestants should include a relatively high proportion of people who report that they are "pleased" at the congregation's integrated status. Those Protestants who would not be pleased simply attend all-white churches.

A final factor associated with acceptance of church integration is the activity of the congregation's clergyman. Respondents were asked whether their clergymen had "taken a public stand in favor of more rights for Negroes." Where the clergymen had taken such a stand, 54 percent of the white respondents reported that they were pleased with the integrated status of the church. Among those who did not know if the clergymen had taken a stand, 41 percent said they were pleased; and among those who reported that the clergymen had not taken a public stand, 34 percent were pleased that both whites and Negroes attended their church. It is tempting to conclude that the clergymen's leadership is the cause behind the parishioners' tolerance toward integration. Yet it is also possible to argue that the line of causality runs the other way—that greater tolerance for integration among a church's members strengthens the inclination of the clergymen to make their views public.

It is also quite possible that the way clergymen are recruited helps explain their views upon, and leadership role concerning, integration. Undoubtedly, a kind of "matching" goes on in the recruitment of clergymen, wherein parishioners call a pastor whose views are similar to their own, and the clergyman himself is likely to accept the invitation of such a congregation. Even where the pastor is assigned by his superiors to a local church, there is some attempt to "match" the leader with his congregation.

INTERRACIAL SOCIAL CONTACTS IN CHURCHES

Those who reported that both whites and Negroes attended their church were asked, "Do white and Negro members mingle much at social affairs, or do both groups keep pretty much to themselves?" Overall, Negroes turned out to be much more likely than whites to report that both races mingle. With the exception of those in Negro segregated neighborhoods, whites in open neighborhoods are slightly more likely than those in other neighborhoods to report social mingling. The differences among the three types of integrated neighborhoods, however, are not striking.

Yet there are some factors that appear conducive to interracial social contacts in the churches. The length of time since integration occurred, for example, is positively related to the degree of reported social contact between the races. Consistent with attitudes toward existing church integration, Protestants are substantially more likely than Catholics to report interracial contact at church functions. Again, it appears that, for Catholics, behavior is influenced by factors other than personal preference. Although Catholics are not enthusiastic about the integration of their congregations, and although they are not as likely as Protestants to come into contact with Negroes in the social life of the church, they do attend integrated churches with comparative frequency. Compared to Protestants, then, it might be said that Catholics are doing it more but enjoying it less.

Finally, the extent of Negro housing demand on the neighborhood, the integration attitudes that already prevail, the respondent's age and educational attainment, and other variables also affect the degree of social contact between the races within churches.

11 *Happiness Is . . .*

IN THIS CHAPTER we discuss a grab bag of miscellaneous neighborhood variables that are, admittedly, not the most important influences on a family's choice of housing or neighborhood. They are, nonetheless, sufficiently important not to ignore. We shall, therefore, examine such things as interracial socializing, recreational facilities, concern about crime, and neighborhood appearance to see how they affect residents' happiness in and with a neighborhood as well as how effective they are in attracting residents to a neighborhood and keeping them there.

Because of socio-economic differences among neighborhoods, we shall generally divide our discussions in this chapter into two parts, treating the high-income and the low-income neighborhoods separately. Thus, we shall compare white segregated, open, and moderately integrated neighborhoods on the one hand and substantially integrated and Negro segregated neighborhoods on the other.

GENERAL HAPPINESS

We shall attempt here to discern neighborhood differences in happiness[1] as related to integrated living. We asked respondents to rate their happiness by answering four questions: How happy are you? How much enjoyment do you get out of life? How well are you doing in getting the things you wanted out of life? How much do you worry?

To the question about happiness, whites in white segregated, open, and moderately integrated neighborhoods all gave roughly the same rating. Answers to the other questions showed that residents of open neighborhoods feel themselves slightly better off than residents of white segregated and moderately integrated neighborhoods, which was almost certainly a consequence of the small differences in median income that characterize these various types of neighborhood.

Negro residents of open and moderately integrated neighborhoods are as happy as, or perhaps a little happier than, their white neighbors. There is, in fact, an indication that Negro residents worry less than whites. However, this difference between whites and Negroes is reversed in substantially integrated neighborhoods, where Negroes are clearly less happy than whites, even when economic variables are controlled. The small fraction of Negroes who have moved into open and moderately integrated neighborhoods may be comparing themselves to all other Negroes and feel relatively gratified both for economic and social reasons.

Comparing whites in substantially integrated neighborhoods with whites in Negro segregated neighborhoods, and Negroes in substantially integrated neighborhoods with Negroes in segregated neighborhoods, one finds no major differences in general happiness, although the Negro responses are consistently less positive than the

[1]The measures of happiness we use are taken from earlier works by Bradburn (Bradburn and Caplovitz, 1965; Bradburn, 1969).

white responses. The small differences between whites in Negro segregated and substantially integrated neighborhoods also indicate that economic factors are more important for happiness than neighborhood factors. If neighborhood factors were important, one might expect white residents of Negro segregated neighborhoods to be less happy, but on three of the four general happiness questions the reverse is true. This is because the income differences favor the white residents of these neighborhoods.

HAPPINESS WITH NEIGHBORHOOD

We asked two questions in order to find out how happy residents were with their neighborhoods: "On the whole, how happy are you living here in (*name of neighborhood*)? Would you say you're very happy, pretty happy, or not too happy with this neighborhood?" and "If, for any reason, you had to move from here to some other neighborhood, would you be very unhappy, a little unhappy, or would you be happy to move—or wouldn't it make any difference?"

The second question was asked because we felt that some residents might be very happy with their neighborhoods, but would think of their residence there as temporary and would not be concerned if they had to move. They might, therefore, have fewer concerns about the neighborhood changing. In fact, the two questions were almost perfectly correlated.

There seem to be no significant differences for whites. Combining the two "unhappy" categories, the percentage of whites who would be unhappy if they were to move ranges from 54 percent in open and Negro segregated neighborhoods to 58 percent in white segregated and substantially integrated neighborhoods. The percentage not too happy with their neighborhood ranges from only 6 to 15 percent. It is clear that in these neighborhoods those white residents who were unhappy with integration have either changed their minds or moved.

Among Negro and white residents in open neighborhoods, there are almost no differences in general satisfaction with the neighborhood. In moderately integrated neighborhoods, Negroes seem a little happier with the neighborhood than whites, but the differences are small. Negroes in open and moderately integrated neighborhoods are more satisfied with their neighborhoods than Negroes in substantially integrated and Negro segregated neighborhoods.

Neighborhood factors do affect the happiness of Negro residents in substantially integrated neighborhoods; they are less happy with their neighborhoods and would be happier to move than Negroes in segregated neighborhoods. A major cause of unhappiness with the neighborhood among Negroes is the reception they faced when the neighborhood was first integrated. Thirty-five percent of the Negro households in substantially integrated neighborhoods where there was panic when the first Negroes moved in are not too happy with their neighborhoods, compared with about 20 percent who are not too happy in neighborhoods where the residents were pleased when integration occurred or where there was no reaction.

The regional differences are striking, but they reflect the same pattern. Only 11 percent of the Negroes in substantially integrated neighborhoods in the South are not too happy with their neighborhoods, compared with 29 percent in the North and West. In the South, where the substantially integrated neighborhoods have been in existence for a long time, Negro residents of these neighborhoods are happier than Negro residents in southern Negro segregated neighborhoods. It is in the North and West that Negroes have felt community displeasure when the neighborhood was integrated. We have no information about community reaction at the time currently Negro segregated neighborhoods were changing, because respondents were not present and could not report what had happened.

Unhappiness with the neighborhood is not related to personal experiences but rather to a poisoned atmosphere that still lingers. Only a few Negro residents reported any specific incidents connected with their own move into the neighborhood; and there is not the consistent relation between length of time in the neighborhood, community reaction when integrated, and happiness with the neighborhood that one would expect if personal experiences were important. Ironically, those white residents who were more responsible for current Negro unhappiness with their neighborhoods have probably moved away, but the ill-feelings still remain.

Another way of measuring Negroes' happiness with the neighborhood is to relate it to their perceptions of neighborhood socializing. We, therefore, asked our Negro respondents: "In general, how often do neighbors get together socially? Would you say often, sometimes, or hardly ever?" In substantially integrated neighborhoods, only 14 percent of the Negro families who say that neighbors sometimes socialize are not happy with their neighborhoods, while 28 percent of those who say that neighbors hardly ever socialize are not too happy.

Actual socializing with neighbors has no apparent effect on happiness with neighborhoods in substantially integrated neighborhoods. Rather, perceived socializing seems to be an item that reflects Negro residents' sense of white neighbors' attitudes toward them. As such, it is, of course, highly influenced by the neighborhood's reaction when the first Negroes moved in.

NEIGHBORING

In contrast to "perceived socializing," how much do white and Negro families *actually* socialize with each other as neighbors, both between races and within their own races? Thus, how much social integration or neighboring really exists? We consider two aspects of neighboring—interracial and general. Since the first accounts for only a small part of total neighboring, general neighboring actually is mostly intra-racial and is basically treated as such here.

In order to measure neighborhood social integration, we asked all the residents in our sample which of six things anyone in their family had done in the past few months with members of families who live in their neighborhood. We asked this question twice, the first time asking about any other families (general neighboring) and the second time asking only about families of the opposite race (interracial neighboring). We shall use here only the responses of whites to the interracial and general neighboring items instead of the responses of both whites and Negroes for two reasons: using both would be in large part redundant since we found no measurable racial differences in general neighboring, and our white sample size is much larger.

Interracial Neighboring

The absolute amount of interracial neighboring in integrated neighborhoods is very low, regardless of the neighborhood's racial balance (Table 11.1). Just because Negroes and whites live near each other does not mean that they see each other socially to any great extent. The small amount of interracial neighborhood socializing that occurs is due primarily to one factor: opportunity—that is, the major determinant of interracial neighboring is the racial composition of the neighborhood. The amount of cross-race neighboring rises mainly as a function of the percentage of Negroes in the neighborhood.

Nevertheless, three other factors, although of secondary importance, do play a role. Whites living in the North and West are more neighborly to Negroes than southern whites are. In the North and West education is positively correlated with interracial neighboring, whereas in the South it is not. Interracial neighborhood socializing is also positively associated with pro-integration attitudes, regardless of region of the country.

General (Intra-racial) Neighboring

The racial composition of a neighborhood has little effect on the extent of neighborhood socializing that takes

Table 11.1 *Interracial Neighboring by Neighborhood Type, for White Residents (Percent Responding "Yes")*

Interracial Neighboring Item	White Segregated	Open	Moderately Integrated	Substantially Integrated	Negro Segregated
			Neighborhood Type		
Stopped and talked when we met	–	10	21	32	37
Had an informal chat together in their home or our home	–	2	5	10	12
Had dinner or a party together at their home or our home	–	1	2	2	1
We got together on other occasions	–	2	3	5	5
Went out together for dinner or a movie	–	1	1	1	1
Attended the meeting of a neighborhood organization or group together	–	3	5	5	2
N	–	(1,099)	(846)	(488)	(108)

place without regard to race. Thus, neighborhood type is not a strong determinant of general (intra-racial) neighboring (Table 11.2); general neighboring is better explained by other factors.

General neighboring is more extensive in the North and West than in the South, in nonmetropolitan areas, among people with more education and higher incomes, among homeowners and in neighborhoods with low Negro housing demand. It is more closely associated with the racial makeup of surrounding areas than with the actual percentage of Negroes in the neighborhoods themselves.

As small as the differences in neighboring by neighborhood type are, they are difficult to explain. In the North and West there is less general neighboring in sub-

Table 11.2 *General Neighboring by Neighborhood Type, for White Residents (Percent Responding "Yes")*

General Neighboring Item	Neighborhood Type				
	White Segre-gated	Open	Moder-ately Inte-grated	Sub-stan-tially Inte-grated	Negro Segre-gated
Stopped and talked when we met	99	92	93	91	94
Had an informal chat together in their home or our home	75	67	67	65	70
Had dinner or a party together at their home or our home	38	34	34	25	36
We got together on other occasions	35	34	26	28	30
Went out together for dinner or a movie	30	30	24	14	24
Attended the meeting of a neighborhood organization or group together	22	23	18	14	22
N	(583)	(1,105)	(866)	(488)	(107)

stantially integrated neighborhoods than in white segregated neighborhoods. General neighboring decreases as the percentage of Negroes in the neighborhood increases, primarily because of the low amount of inter-racial neighboring. From white segregated to substantially integrated neighborhoods, there is a trend toward decreasing neighboring in the North and West. Strictly speaking, the trend seems to disappear under many control conditions, but the breakdown is more apparent than real. Very often it is because the percentage of Negroes in open and moderately integrated neighborhoods is not too dif-ferent. If these two types of neighborhoods are considered to be virtually equivalent in proportion of Negroes, then the trend is sharper.

To the extent that there are differences in general neighboring by neighborhood type, they must be specified. White segregated neighborhoods are more neighborly than substantially integrated neighborhoods in the North and West; the opposite may be true of the South. The differences in the North and West become more marked as family income increases, and the argument is limited mainly to homeowners.

RECREATIONAL FACILITIES

We do not have enough recreational facilities in the area. The dissatisfaction is not with those we have, but because we don't have enough.

They don't have any recreational facilities in the area so they just play in the street.

There is nothing there except the steam bath, and you wouldn't call that neighborhood recreation.
Informants in white segregated neighborhoods

We have more beautiful parks than anywhere in the world. One is in a canyon with waterfalls.
Informant in integrated neighborhood

No one lives in a house solely because it is near a park or YMCA, but the presence and condition of such recreational facilities are of some importance, all else being equal.

There are no absolute measures of the quality of neighborhood facilities. We have been reasonably confident when the ratings of informants and residents agreed, but how does one explain the discrepancies between them? We would suggest that there are residual tensions in those neighborhoods where there were tensions when the neighborhoods first became integrated that tend to distort residents' perceptions of their neighborhoods. Negro residents and, to a lesser extent, white residents project their unhappiness with their neighborhoods onto neighborhood facilities; and, hence, their evaluations may not be entirely accurate. On the other hand, since informants' responses are less likely to be affected by neighborhood tensions, they may be considered reasonably valid.

The residents and informants in white segregated, open, and moderately integrated neighborhoods consistently rated their recreational facilities about half-way between above average and average, with one exception. The children's facilities in moderately integrated neighborhoods were rated above average or superior. Informants in white segregated, open, and moderately integrated neighborhoods believe that about one-third of all of the recreational facilities have an important effect on keeping residents in or attracting new residents to their neighborhoods. In substantially integrated and Negro segregated neighborhoods, one-fourth of the facilities were rated as similarly important.

Dissatisfactions with Recreational Facilities

A major difference between white segregated neighborhoods and open and moderately integrated neighborhoods appears in response to the question asked of residents. "Are you or your family dissatisfied with the recreational facilities here?" and the question asked of neighborhood informants, "What *dissatisfactions* have there been with community recreational facilities recently?" Both residents and informants of open and moderately integrated neighborhoods report more dissatisfaction with recreational facilities than residents and informants in white segregated neighborhoods. Thirty-one percent of the residents of moderately integrated neighborhoods are dissatisfied, compared with 24 percent in white segregated neighborhoods. The differences are even greater among informants. In both open and moderately integrated areas, 75 percent of the informants report some dissatisfaction among residents, compared with 62 percent in white segregated neighborhoods.

Dissatisfaction with recreational facilities is, of course, closely related to the presence or absence of children. Even when this factor is controlled, however, residents in open and moderately integrated neighborhoods are still more dissatisfied with their recreational facilities. Although it seems possible that differences in the levels of dissatisfaction are due to differences between central cities and suburbs, such is not the case. Controlling for urbanization, the differences between open and moderately integrated and white segregated neighborhoods remain.

The chief cause of dissatisfaction among residents is the perceived absence of facilities, especially public facilities. This difference seems to be in the use of public and private facilities. Residents of integrated neighborhoods expect more of public recreational facilities because they use them more often than residents of white segregated neighborhoods, who use private facilities more. About 85 percent of the households in open and moderately integrated neighborhoods use public recreational facilities, compared with 75 percent of the households in white segregated neighborhoods.

White residents in substantially integrated and Negro segregated neighborhoods (the low-income neighborhoods) are no less satisfied with recreational facilities than the residents of the high-income neighborhoods. Negro residents, however, are less satisfied, especially in substantially integrated neighborhoods. The reverse is the case for informants—those in substantially integrated neighborhoods are less likely to report dissatisfactions with recreational facilities than those in Negro segregated neighborhoods.

Integration of Recreational Facilities

Another major difference between the recreational facilities in integrated and segregated neighborhoods is in their use by both Negroes and whites. Public recreational facilities in open and moderately integrated neighborhoods are highly integrated, with 82 percent of the facilities in open neighborhoods and 93 percent of the facilities in moderately integrated neighborhoods used by both Negroes and whites, compared with 48 percent in white segregated neighborhoods.

Integrated usage differences are smaller for private facilities, but in the same direction. In moderately integrated neighborhoods, 79 percent of the private recreational facilities are used by both races, compared with 50 percent in open and 41 percent in white segregated neighborhoods. More than any other neighborhood institution, recreational facilities are the most heavily used by both races.

When we consider the low-income neighborhoods, the available recreational facilities in substantially integrated neighborhoods are far more likely to be integrated than the facilities in Negro segregated neighborhoods. A little over half the public facilities and 39 percent of the private facilities are integrated in Negro segregated neighborhoods. These percentages are almost identical to the ones for white segregated neighborhoods.

It is not so surprising that the level of integration in all recreational facilities is lower in substantially integrated neighborhoods than in moderately integrated neighborhoods, since white residents in substantially integrated neighborhoods have the least favorable attitudes toward integration. When Negroes begin to use facilities too much, whites tend to stop using them. Private facilities, on the other hand, are most integrated in substantially integrated neighborhoods, where 69 percent are used by both Negroes and whites, 26 percent by only whites, and 5 percent by only Negroes.

Teenage Use of Recreational Facilities

A source of major dissatisfaction with recreational facilities is the lack of such facilities and their accompanying services for teenagers. Over and over again there were comments such as these:

> There is no program at all for the teenage group. That is the big problem in this neighborhood. The kids just don't know what to do with themselves. Clustering in a discon-

tented fashion with nothing to do. For instance they will show up with soft drinks they've gotten at the store and break the bottles on trees or benches or each other. The teenage problem is big enough to make up for the lack of any others.

There's just nothing for teenagers. There's an area in the back of the park for toddlers, and an area in front for old people. The city fathers just spent $30,000 last year removing the trees and shrubs from the area. I know why they did it. They wanted to keep kids from hiding in the bushes. But now if the people living next to the park see kids playing ball in the park or making the slightest bit of noise, the police come and throw the kids out. They're not supposed to play ball you see, but kids are normal and like to play ball and make noise. It's part of growing up. The schools have gyms that could be used for dances and other activities, but they won't open them up. They're afraid they wouldn't be able to handle the kids.

The lack of teenage recreational facilities is cited by informants in both integrated and segregated neighborhoods, but more often by informants in integrated neighborhoods. In addition, teenage rowdiness, gang fights, and vandalism are mentioned more often by informants in integrated neighborhoods:

Families are annoyed with the dance night. They object to the noise. This summer there was quite a bit of difficulty in the park program. There was an incident of a knife fight. The trouble was mostly caused by outsiders—not our own kids. They come over from another part of town just looking for trouble. We had to cancel dances.

While the above remark about outsiders may be part of the general tendency to blame trouble on the other guy, there is some validity to it, particularly in central cities. We suspect that many of the open and moderately integrated areas in central cities are near enough to low socio-economic neighborhoods so that teenagers from the latter areas often share recreational facilities with the former, especially since facilities in the low-class neighborhoods are so inadequate. This practice leads to over-crowding of facilities in the open and moderately in-tegrated neighborhoods and, often, to tension. This ten-sion is sometimes racial if the outsiders are Negroes; but the same kind of tension has existed for decades among white teenage ethnic groups. The white segregated neigh-borhoods are usually farther from these low-class neigh-borhoods, and hence less affected by the same kinds of pressures.

NEIGHBORHOOD CRIME

Crime is an important concern in many neighborhoods, particularly those in the central cities of metropolitan areas. There is also a significant link between teenage delinquency and the recreational facilities most frequently used by teenagers.

Both residents and informants of open and moderately integrated neighborhoods indicate somewhat more con-cern about crime than do residents and informants in white segregated neighborhoods (Table 11.3). Concern is most heavily concentrated in central cities of metropolitan areas. The greatest difference in central cities is between residents in open neighborhoods, 23 percent of whom are very worried about crime, and residents in white segregated neighborhoods, only 11 percent of whom are worried.

We cannot explain why residents of moderately in-tegrated neighborhoods are less fearful of crime than resi-dents in open neighborhoods except to note that our infor-mation is not based on actual crime statistics but on resi-dents' conceptions of the current prevalence of crime and their concerns about the future.

There are no major differences in concern about crime between residents in substantially integrated and Negro segregated neighborhoods; the level of concern is about the same as in open and moderately integrated neigh-borhoods. Residents in substantially integrated neigh-

Table 11.3 *Concern About Crime, by Neighborhood Type (Percent of Households: Data from Residents or Informants As Indicated)*

Item	White Segregated	Open	Moderately Integrated	Substantially Integrated	Negro Segregated
Residents' attitude toward neighborhood crime situation:					
Very worried	8	15	12	17	15
A little worried	35	37	34	32	36
Not at all worried	57	48	54	51	49
Total	100	100	100	100	100
Informants' reports about neighborhood crime situation:					
Very worried	17	24	24	37	39
A little worried	48	49	51	37	32
Not at all worried	35	27	25	26	29
Total	100	100	100	100	100

borhoods are a little more likely to be very worried about the crime situation than any of the other residents, but a majority of them are not at all worried.

A significant difference between the responses of the informants in the low and in the high socio-economic neighborhoods is discernible, however. Informants in substantially integrated and Negro segregated neighborhoods are much more likely to report that residents are very worried about crime than informants in white segregated, open, and moderately integrated neighborhoods. This difference corresponds with available crime statistics that show a substantially higher rate of crime in low-income neighborhoods than in high-income neighborhoods. Since informants are more aware of what is happening in a neighborhood, their reports should correlate more closely with crime statistics than the reports of individual residents.

Common Types of Crime

We asked neighborhood informants and residents to tell us which of the following common types of crime they thought occurred most often in their neighborhoods: general rowdiness, vandalism, and fights; robberies and burglaries; and major crimes, such as assault and battery, rape, and murder. Residents in white segregated, open, and moderately integrated neighborhoods all agree that robberies and burglaries are the most frequently committed crimes, while major crimes occur very seldom.

Whites in substantially integrated and Negro segregated neighborhoods report a higher proportion of major crimes than residents of the high-income neighborhoods, but they report about the same proportion of general rowdiness and vandalism. Among Negroes, those in substantially integrated neighborhoods are more likely than those in Negro segregated neighborhoods to complain of rowdiness, fights, or vandalism. On the other hand, Negroes in segregated neighborhoods are more likely to mention robberies and burglaries. Perhaps some of the fights in substantially integrated neighborhoods could be the result of interracial friction between teenagers. Among informants, however, there are only minor differences in the types of crime mentioned by neighborhood.

To summarize, concern about crime probably does not influence many housing decisions. In response to an open-ended question about "the three or four most important problems of the neighborhood," only 5 percent of the residents in open neighborhoods and 4 percent in moderately integrated neighborhoods considered crime the most serious neighborhood problem, compared with 2 percent of the residents in white segregated neighborhoods. Still, those respondents who are concerned about crime have very deep feelings, as was made clear by a priest in a moderately integrated neighborhood:

> Crime is absolutely the number one problem, and we're sick and tired of everyone saying "our hands are tied."

Who tied them? That includes everyone from the mayor, the judges, the police, the school principals on down. It's time they started doing something.

PHYSICAL APPEARANCE OF NEIGHBORHOOD

About half of both the residents and the informants in white segregated, open, and moderately integrated neighborhoods rate the physical appearance of their neighborhoods above average or superior. The white residents of Negro segregated neighborhoods rate their neighborhoods' appearance slightly higher than the white residents of substantially integrated neighborhoods, but the ratings of informants in these neighborhoods turn out to be just the reverse. Both informants and Negro residents in substantially integrated neighborhoods rate their neighborhoods higher in physical appearance than informants and Negro residents in Negro segregated neighborhoods, but the differences are small. Among residents, only about 30 percent of the whites and only 15 percent of the Negroes in substantially integrated or Negro segregated neighborhoods rate the physical appearance of their neighborhoods as above average or superior.

TRANSPORTATION FACILITIES

The availability of public transportation facilities is no longer important for most wage earners. In our sample, only about one in ten residents uses public transportation to go to work; about three out of four drive; and the remainder walk to work or work at home. In open neighborhoods, 20 percent of the household heads use public transportation, suggesting that these are residents of New York City and the other large cities with subway systems.

The private car is almost as ubiquitous in substantially integrated and Negro segregated neighborhoods as in white segregated, open, and moderately integrated neighborhoods. Eighty-one percent of the white wage earners and 65 percent of the Negro wage earners in substantially integrated neighborhoods go to work in a private car. The proportions are a little higher for whites and Negroes in Negro segregated neighborhoods. The median time required for whites in both substantially integrated and Negro segregated neighborhoods to get to work is fourteen minutes, which is only slightly less than the time required for those in the high-income neighborhoods. The median traveling time for Negroes is about five minutes longer, primarily because more Negroes take public transportation or walk to work.

These results provide no evidence that families live in substantially integrated neighborhoods to save travel time. Rather they suggest that the average wage earner in our sample is willing to spend about fifteen to twenty minutes a day getting to work and looks for housing (or a job) that meets this requirement.

SUMMARY

Overall, then, we find no differences among whites in the general satisfactions of living in integrated and segregated neighborhoods. On the other hand, Negroes in substantially integrated neighborhoods who faced hostile neighborhood reaction when they moved in are less happy with their neighborhoods and more willing to move out than Negroes who did not face any hostility or who moved into a segregated Negro neighborhood. Negroes in open and moderately integrated neighborhoods, however, are as happy as, or even a little happier than, their white neighbors.

Happiness in neighborhoods is not related to neighborhood socializing. The absolute amount of interracial neighboring in integrated neighborhoods is very low, mainly limited to saying hello when Negro and white neighbors meet. General (intra-racial) socializing is much heavier, but is not highly related to the level of integration in the neighborhood.

The availability and use of recreational facilities is about the same for white segregated, open, and moderately integrated neighborhoods. Residents of integrated neighborhoods are more likely, however, to use public facilities, while in white segregated neighborhoods there is greater use of private facilities. There are no major differences in the facilities of substantially integrated and Negro segregated neighborhoods; but, since these two neighborhoods have markedly lower incomes per household than the other neighborhoods, they are likely to have poorer community services and recreational facilities.

Residents of integrated neighborhoods are slightly more worried about crime than residents of other neighborhoods. This is mainly true in the central cities of metropolitan areas, although a little of this fear of crime is also seen in integrated suburbs. Some of this fear reflects the proximity of lower-class neighborhoods, while some may again be a manifestation of general neighborhood worries in integrated areas. There are no objective measures of crime in these neighborhoods, so one cannot separate unfounded from well-founded worries.

Except for those based on economic differences, reports about the physical appearance of integrated and segregated neighborhoods do not differ. Finally, the small differences in the availability of public transportation also appear to have no effect on neighborhood integration.

12 The Future of Integrated Neighborhoods in America

I have a dream that my four little children will one day live in a nation where they will not be judged by the color of their skin but by the content of their character.

I have a dream today.

Martin Luther King, Jr.
Lincoln Memorial,
Washington, D.C.
August 28, 1963

ONE OF FIVE Americans lives in integrated surroundings. It would be gratifying to predict that this proportion will rise steadily and substantially in the years ahead. Unfortunately, the results of our research are not clear enough to enable us to make this prediction. At best, we anticipate rather modest increases in the number of integrated neighborhoods and in the proportion of the population living in these neighborhoods in the next decade.

There are several trends operating simultaneously. In white segregated neighborhoods, there will be small but steady integration, particularly in those neighborhoods most like the ones that are currently integrated. In open and moderately integrated neighborhoods, there will be moderate increases in the proportion of Negroes. Substantially integrated neighborhoods, however, face the pressures of an ever increasing Negro population, and some will slowly become Negro segregated.

In the search for a villain, there is a great temptation to blame the white families who move out of integrated neighborhoods for the resegregation of these neighborhoods. These are not always families who have panicked, however, but rather families who have moved mainly because of changes in jobs or family composition, or because their friends and relatives are now living elsewhere. At the same time, the pent-up Negro demand for housing in these neighborhoods is greater than white demand; this demand differential is chiefly responsible for slow neighborhood resegregation.

The higher the current proportion of Negroes is in a neighborhood, and the nearer the neighborhood is to other Negro segregated neighborhoods, the greater are the residents' concerns about the neighborhood changing. Only in the South, where there is no social integration but where housing integration is longstanding, are the current neighborhood proportion of Negroes and distance to Negro areas wholly unrelated to stability.

There is no way of knowing which white segregated neighborhoods will become integrated in the next few years, but we asked neighborhood residents to predict the likelihood of their areas becoming integrated. Those neighborhoods in which residents were more favorable to integration were also the ones that residents predicted would be most likely to become integrated.

These results are by no means symmetrical. Most white segregated neighborhoods do not adjoin all-Negro areas, while many substantially integrated neighborhoods do. Thus, whether a white segregated neighborhood becomes integrated, remains segregated, or panics and becomes a changing neighborhood depends primarily on the attitudes and characteristics of its residents. Conversely, whether a stable integrated neighborhood ultimately becomes a resegregated Negro neighborhood depends primarily on the Negro housing demand from adjoining areas.

These modest predictions assume that the rise in pro-integration sentiments over the last several decades will continue, and that there will be no major changes in government policies at the national or local levels. We believe that integration could be accelerated if successful programs were developed to:

1. Raise the income level of Negro families;
2. Improve financing opportunities for Negroes trying to buy homes;
3. Increase the heterogeneity of housing in suburban neighborhoods by building both owner and rental housing units in different price ranges; and
4. Remove discriminatory barriers in currently white segregated neighborhoods against renting by Negro families.

Now that baseline measures of the extent of integration in the United States have been established, we hope that it will be possible to repeat this study periodically in order to measure changes resulting from the factors that we have discussed: government policies, legal and moral pressures, changing attitudes, and the rise in the socio-economic status of Negroes. Although annual changes would be small, we would expect to detect significant changes over periods of from three to five years.

CONCERNS ABOUT NEIGHBORHOOD CHANGING

Our informants did not expect any of the integrated neighborhoods in this study to become changing or Negro segregated neighborhoods within the next five years. Nevertheless, it seems likely that, through a slow attrition process whereby the white market gradually dries up, some of these neighborhoods will ultimately change. The best indications we have that this may happen are the responses we received from the white residents of integrated neighborhoods when we asked them: "Are people around here very concerned about the neighborhood changing, a little concerned, or not concerned at all?" The best measure we have of neighborhood informants' concern about racial

change are their responses to these two questions: "I would
like your best guess as to whether during the next five
years you think this neighborhood will remain about as it
is, or will it change in some ways?" and "In five years, what
do you think the proportion of Negroes in this neighborhood might be?"

Residents' concerns and informants' predictions about
their neighborhoods changing show that there is more concern in substantially integrated neighborhoods than in
moderately integrated and open neighborhoods. Residents
in substantially integrated neighborhoods in central cities
and in the North and West are the most likely to be concerned about their neighborhoods changing. In the South,
however, residents of substantially integrated neighborhoods have little concern about neighborhood change
because there is a long history of stable integrated housing.
Even in the North and West, residents who are very concerned about their neighborhoods changing are in the minority. About 40 percent of the residents of substantially
integrated neighborhoods, 25 percent in moderately integrated neighborhoods, and 20 percent in open neighborhoods are very concerned.

These concerns are mainly related to the Negro housing
demand that residents feel from adjacent neighborhoods.
The greater the maximum percentage of Negroes—*not* the
average percentage—in any adjacent neighborhood, the
greater the concern about neighborhood change. Among
residents of open neighborhoods, concern about the neighborhood changing rises slightly but steadily from 18 to 26
percent as the maximum percentage of Negroes in adjacent neighborhoods goes from 0 to 50 percent or more.
In substantially integrated neighborhoods, which are
much more likely to be adjacent to a neighborhood that
has a high proportion of Negroes, this high proportion
does not seem to have any effect. The greatest effect is in
moderately integrated neighborhoods where the proportion of households concerned about the neighborhood
changing more than doubles from 18 to 38 percent when

the maximum percentage of Negroes in adjacent neighborhoods is more than 30 percent.

Another indication of Negro demand for housing in a neighborhood is its distance from the nearest Negro segregated neighborhood. As the distance increases, fewer residents are concerned about the neighborhood changing. In substantially integrated neighborhoods, 40 percent of the residents in neighborhoods a mile or less from an all-Negro neighborhood are concerned about their neighborhoods changing. The percentage of concerned residents decreases substantially in neighborhoods two or more miles from the nearest Negro neighborhood (though the sizes of our samples are perhaps too small to permit reliable percentaging). Among moderately integrated neighborhoods, the percentage who are concerned drops from 32 percent in neighborhoods a mile or less from Negro neighborhoods to 10 percent in neighborhoods more than five miles away from the nearest Negro area. The trend in open neighborhoods is not clear, but even here there is a drop in concern if the neighborhood is more than a mile from the nearest Negro neighborhood.

The racial composition of the new residents moving into the neighborhood also affects concern about neighborhood change. The major differences occur in moderately integrated neighborhoods. If 70 percent or more of the new residents are white, then only 19 percent of the residents are concerned about the neighborhood changing; while if 40–69 percent of the new residents are white, then 55 percent of the residents are concerned. A smaller difference in the same direction is observed in substantially integrated neighborhoods. There are no open or moderately integrated neighborhoods where the current percentage of whites moving in is less than 40 percent.

Neighborhood Change and Integration Attitudes

For integrated neighborhoods where the Negro housing demand is high—that is, the ones most likely to change—there is no relation between concern and integration attitudes. In moderately integrated neighborhoods where the Negro housing demand is medium, there is a substantial difference among residents with low attitudes toward integration and those with medium or high attitudes. (Some of the variation may be due merely to the small sample sizes since, controlling for region, demand, and attitudes, many of the percentages are based on only twenty or thirty cases.) There does seem to be a pattern: those residents who hold a very low view of integration move from an integrated neighborhood soon after the first Negro families move in and long before there is any real basis for concern about the neighborhood changing. By the time the possibility of neighborhood change is real, the strong anti-integrationists have either left or their views have been modified by living in an integrated atmosphere. Thus, realistic concerns are not closely related to current anti-integration attitudes. Generally, the whites who remain are less prejudiced than the ones who moved.

Concerns About Neighborhood Changing, by Ownership Status

One characteristic of a neighborhood that makes change more likely is the availability of rental units. In open and moderately integrated neighborhoods, renters are more likely to be concerned about the neighborhood changing than owners. In open neighborhoods, 24 percent of all of the renters and only 16 percent of all of the owners are concerned. In moderately integrated neighborhoods, 28 percent of the renters and 21 percent of the owners are concerned. Only in substantially integrated neighborhoods are the differences trivial.

These concerns would appear to be contrary to the theory we developed earlier, suggesting that substantially integrated neighborhoods with many rental units were the most likely to change, and that it would be easier for Negro families to move into open and moderately integrated neighborhoods with rental units. One explanation of this ostensible paradox might be the relation between integration attitudes and ownership status. Renters are more likely to have low or medium integration attitudes because of their lower incomes, and this could lead to greater concerns about the neighborhood changing. Only in substantially integrated neighborhoods among residents who have low integration attitudes are owners more concerned than renters. While we have no explanation for this reversal, a hindsight explanation for the generally greater concern by renters suggests itself. We suspect, but have no data to confirm this, that renters' concerns are related to a feeling of *powerlessness*. The renter has no voice in determining whether the landlord will or will not rent to Negroes; he can play no part in an owner's decision to sell or not sell his house. He is like the car passenger whose life is in the hands of the driver, and who is far more nervous than the driver.

POSSIBLE INTEGRATION OF WHITE SEGREGATED NEIGHBORHOODS

There are three long-range possibilities for neighborhoods that are currently white segregated. They can remain segregated, become integrated, or change to Negro segregated. In order to predict their future, neighborhoods may be measured in two ways. The first measures the integration attitudes of the residents. It might be expected that the probability of a segregated neighborhood becoming integrated would be positively correlated with favorable attitudes toward integration. The second measures housing market characteristics in the neighborhood and in adjacent neighborhoods. The greater the Negro housing demand in the neighborhood, the more likely Negroes are to move in.

The connection between high demand and anti-integration attitudes could cause a neighborhood to become Negro segregated without ever first being integrated. Anti-integration attitudes would initially lead to such "keep-them-out" tactics as vandalism and rioting, which ultimately are not likely to be successful. These acts, however, would frighten away white buyers and renters, making it impossible for the neighborhood to become integrated. While our findings are not as conclusive as these statements, they nevertheless tend to support them.

Our prediction of change in the racial composition of the white segregated neighborhoods is based on the following question asked of white residents: "Is there any possibility of a Negro family moving into this neighborhood in the next few years?" The use of the words "any possibility" increases the proportion of "yes" answers, and for all white segregated neighborhoods, 37 percent of the respondents answered "yes." If one believed this answer, then one could predict that roughly 16 million more white households would be living in integrated neighborhoods in the next few years. Yet this estimate is probably too high. For one thing, it ignores the financial and social factors that would prevent many Negro families from moving into these neighborhoods even if housing were available. For another, it ignores the likelihood that some of these neighborhoods would change from white to Negro segregated after the first Negro families moved in. While the figure of 37 percent cannot be taken literally, it does indicate that many white families can at least conceive of the idea of Negroes in their neighborhoods. Although we have no trend data, it seems reasonable to conjecture that this estimate is substantially higher than it would have been a decade or two ago.

Relation of Possible Integration of Segregated Neighborhoods to Housing Market and Demand from Adjacent Neighborhoods

As might be expected, the housing market affects the possibility of Negroes moving into a neighborhood. In order to determine the characteristics of the market, we asked neighborhood informants whether it was easier or harder to sell a house now than five years ago. Only 23 percent of the residents in neighborhoods where informants say it is easier to sell a house think there is a possibility of Negroes moving in during the next few years, while 43 percent of the residents in neighborhoods where houses are harder to sell think this is a possibility.

Surprisingly, in the residents' predictions, Negro housing demand seems to have no apparent connection with the possibility that Negroes will move into the neighborhood. But among residents with low and medium integration attitudes, as the Negro demand rises, so does the percentage who think there is a possibility that Negroes will move in. Among residents with high integration attitudes, demand has only a small effect. As Negro demand rises from low to high, the predicted average proportion of Negroes in five years, based on responses from the neighborhood informants, rises from 1 to 11 percent.

There is an interesting difference between residents in open and white segregated neighborhoods. In open neighborhoods, residents with low integration attitudes are much more concerned about neighborhood change than residents with high integration attitudes, but in white segregated neighborhoods, residents with low integration attitudes express the belief that their neighborhood will remain segregated.

It seems that those neighborhoods where the Negro housing demand is high and where residents do not see the possibility of Negroes moving in are, in fact, the ones most likely to change to Negro segregated. In contrast, areas where residents have anti-integration attitudes and Negro housing demand is low are likely to remain white segregated. If the demand is low and residents are pro-integration, the area could eventually become integrated, although *when* this occurs depends on whether Negro families can afford the price of housing in the area. If demand is high and residents are pro-integration, then there is a high probability that Negro families will move into the neighborhood soon. Yet these newly integrated neighborhoods may also face the possibility of becoming resegregated.

Relation Between Possible Integration of Segregated Neighborhoods and Integration Attitudes

One would also think that white residents with high integration attitudes would be more likely to expect Negroes to move into their neighborhoods. In part, this may reflect a wish for integration, but it may also reflect the fact that Negro families are willing to move into a neighborhood where they are accepted or welcomed. Table 12.1 shows that 62 percent of the residents of white segregated neighborhoods who hold high integration attitudes expect Negro families to move into their neighborhoods in the

Table 12.1 *Percent of Households in White Segregated Neighborhoods Who Think There Is a Chance of Negroes Moving into Their Neighborhoods in Next Few Years, by Integration Attitudes, Perceived Personal and Community Reaction, and Religious Variety in Neighborhoods, for the United States and by Region*

		Region	
Item	U.S.	North and West	South
Integration attitudes:			
Low	23 (209)	21 (129)	21 (80)
Medium	38 (175)	39 (154)	34 (121)
High	62 (105)	63 (101)	*[a] (4)
Personal reaction:			
Not concerned	44 (231)	47 (201)	27 (30)
Concerned—Would not move	30 (253)	31 (179)	29 (75)
Concerned—Would move	27 (63)	23 (35)	31 (28)
Perceived community reaction:			
None	47 (49)	46 (46)	* (4)
Gossip	40 (218)	43 (161)	31 (56)
Panic or violence	35 (131)	40 (87)	23 (38)
Religious variety in neighborhood:			
Low	39 (206)	35 (52)	21 (73)
Medium	41 (248)	42 (224)	32 (24)
High	27 (125)	36 (98)	* (8)

[a]Asterisks indicate too few cases for reliable percentaging.

next few years, compared with 23 percent of the residents who have low integration attitudes.

Other attitudes that are related to integration expectations are perceived personal and community reactions to Negroes moving in. Among the residents who would not be personally concerned, 44 percent think there is a possibility of a Negro family moving in during the next few years; among the residents who say they would move out if Negroes move in, only 27 percent think that Negroes might indeed move in. Among the residents who think that there would be no community reaction if Negro families moved in, 47 percent think that there is a chance of this happening, while 35 percent of the residents who predict community panic or violence think that Negroes will move in.

PREDICTED FUTURE FOR WHITE
SEGREGATED NEIGHBORHOODS

The broad predictions made here about the future of white segregated neighborhoods in the next decade are based upon the distribution of white segregated neighborhoods in the United States and in the North and West in terms of Negro housing demand and integration attitudes (Table 12.2). The South is excluded since our sample of white segregated neighborhoods there is so small, but there is no evidence that, in this regard, southern segregated neighborhoods are much different from those elsewhere.

About one-quarter of the residents in white segregated neighborhoods have high integration attitudes, and we would predict that roughly this same proportion will, in the next decade or two, live in neighborhoods that are integrated. This is less than the 37 percent of the residents who believe that there is a possibility that Negroes will move into their neighborhoods, but in absolute numbers it is still more than ten million households. Based on our conclusions about currently integrated neighborhoods, we

Table 12.2 *Distribution of White Segregated Neighborhoods in the United States and in the North and West, by Negro Housing Demand and Integration Attitudes (Percent of Households)*

Integration Attitudes	U. S.	North and West
	Low Negro Housing Demand	
Low	16	20
Medium	16	21
High	13	18
	Medium Negro Housing Demand	
Low	14	10
Medium	11	12
High	13	5
	High Negro Housing Demand	
Low	9	4
Medium	6	7
High	2	3
Total	100	100
N	(537)	(382)

would guess that, of this number, from 5 to 10 percent (.5 to 1 million households) would live in neighborhoods that might ultimately change again from integrated to Negro segregated.

About 10 percent of the residents (four million households) who have low integration attitudes live in neighborhoods where Negro housing demand is high—areas that are likely to become changing neighborhoods in the next two decades. The remaining 65 percent of the residents (25 million households) will continue to live in white segregated neighborhoods.

Underlying these predictions are many assumptions, probably the most important being that the attitudes of all of the residents of white segregated neighborhoods over the next two decades will become like the current attitudes in our special sample of control neighborhoods. Our segregated neighborhoods were chosen to be similar to our sample of integrated neighborhoods and, therefore, they are above average in socio-economic level. The residents of these segregated control neighborhoods are thus more pro-integration than all of the residents of white segregated neighborhoods.

Far better predictions of neighborhood change will be possible when another study of integrated neighborhoods has been completed, one showing not only the gross changes in all neighborhoods, but the factors that relate to changes in the status of specific neighborhoods. Still, one major point needs to be made: there are currently some white segregated neighborhoods that are receptive to integration and will eventually become integrated.

The personal reactions of residents and the perceived reactions of the community to the possibility of Negroes moving in provide still another indication of the readiness of some white segregated neighborhoods to accept Negroes. About half of the residents of white segregated neighborhoods said that they would not be concerned if Negroes moved in. About one in eight would be concerned but would not move, one in four might move, and the balance would move. Those who expressed concern were mainly worried about a decrease in property values or neighborhood deterioration. The chief form of community reaction would be gossip, which was mentioned by almost half of the respondents. About 30 percent thought that there would be some panic or decisive action against the Negro families. Positive reactions were mentioned by only 2 percent of the respondents. The impression left by these figures is hardly one of eagerness to integrate segregated neighborhoods but rather one of acceptance of the event after it occurs.

PREDICTED RACIAL COMPOSITION OF NEIGHBORHOODS IN 1972

The replies of our neighborhood informants indicate that the proportion of Negro residents will have increased in each type of neighborhood by 1972. In open and moderately integrated neighborhoods, the predicted increases are modest: a 5 percent median increase in open neighborhoods and a 7 percent median increase in moderately integrated neighborhoods. A major increase is predicted in substantially integrated neighborhoods in the North and West, with the percentage of Negroes doubling to 40 percent. The data are too sparse to predict changes in substantially integrated neighborhoods in the South, but increases there will probably be smaller than in the North and West. We do not predict that any Negro segregated neighborhoods will become integrated, although this has happened in a few areas, particularly where new housing has attracted whites.

Neighborhood informants believe that 85 percent of households in white segregated neighborhoods will have Negro families living in the same neighborhood with them within the next five years, although the median percentage of Negroes will still be only 1 percent. This is a higher estimate than either the residents or we predict. This prediction, rather than being a realistic appraisal, probably reflects either the pro-integration sentiments of the informants or the desire on their part not to appear bigoted. We agree with our neighborhood informants' overall prediction, but we think that they have been optimistic about the time it will take. The proportion of Negro households in open and moderately integrated neighborhoods will rise slowly with little fuss being made. In northern and western substantially integrated neighborhoods, there will be a more rapid increase in the Negro population, but some of these neighborhoods will become resegregated. More white segregated neighborhoods will get their first Negro families, and in most cases there will be no major reactions. Where there are strong reactions, the neighborhood will probably become a changing or Negro segregated one. Most white segregated neighborhoods, however, will remain segregated for the foreseeable future.

Description of Sampling
and Classification Procedures

SEVERAL different kinds of samples were used in our study of integrated neighborhoods; each will be discussed separately here. In general, the samples meet the following key requirements:

1. The sample of white residents in integrated neighborhoods is a self-weighting probability sample of all white residents in such neighborhoods.

2. The sample of Negro residents in integrated neighborhoods is a self-weighting probability sample of all Negro residents in such neighborhoods.

3. Since the Negro sample is selected at a rate 2.5 times that of the white sample, a weighted sample of *all* residents in integrated neighborhoods is obtained by multiplying the white sample results by 2.5 or, conversely, the Negro sample by .4.

4. The control samples of whites and Negroes living in segregated white or Negro neighborhoods are *not* representative of all residents living in such areas. They were selected to match the residents of integrated neighborhoods as closely as possible so that differences between integrated and segregated neighborhoods would not be due to geography, income, or type of dwelling, but, rather, to the residual differences between the two.

5. The integrated neighborhoods in this study are not a

simple random sample of neighborhoods, but, rather, they were selected with probabilities proportionate to the size of the neighborhood. Thus, those results that depend only on the number or percentage of neighborhoods with a given characteristic require that the neighborhoods be weighted inversely to their sizes. The unweighted data produce results about the number or percentage of residents in neighborhoods with a given attribute.

LOCATION OF INTEGRATED NEIGHBORHOODS, PHASE I

The primary sampling units (PSUs) are those in the National Opinion Research Center's basic national sample (1962) that was based on the 1960 census and on estimated population growth between 1960 and 1970. Each of about 17,000 census tracts or enumeration districts was classified by NORC interviewers as containing or not containing an integrated neighborhood. This was determined by interviewing more than 3,500 respondents in the NORC primary sampling areas. The interviewers started with city-wide informants who had a broad knowledge of the housing patterns in the entire area. We found the following organizations to be especially useful in supplying informants for this study:

County and city commissions on human or race relations
Metropolitan planning commissions
Chambers of commerce
Fair housing commissions
Federal housing authorities
Urban renewal or development boards
State or local real estate associations
NAACPs
Urban Leagues
Conferences on race and religion
Local councils of churches
School administrations
Local newspapers
Realtor associations
Banks
Postal officials
Police officials

Generally, these informants also knew the names of other people who would be knowledgeable about integration. This "snowball" sampling procedure is particularly appropriate for obtaining the most complete information at the lowest cost.

Interviewers were told to get information for each census tract or group of tracts or from at least two different informants, and more if there were disagreements. Generally, the informants were church leaders, heads of settlement houses, school officials, and members of community organizations. Their information about the local neighborhoods was usually accurate, although they were not always aware of all of the integrated neighborhoods. Of course, not all interviews were equally productive—some yielded very detailed information about an area; others produced nothing more useful than the name of a more knowledgeable informant.

SAMPLING OF INTEGRATED NEIGHBORHOODS, PHASE II

Early in our planning of this project we had decided that a large number of sample neighborhoods would be needed because of the diversity of neighborhood types: a sample of roughly 200 integrated neighborhoods and 100 control neighborhoods seemed optimal.

Using the results of Phase I—the location of integrated neighborhoods—we estimated that there were about 8,750,000 U.S. households located in census tracts which contained an integrated neighborhood. (This estimate proved to be low.) With only the data from Phase I to go on, we could not know the exact sizes of the integrated neighborhoods. We, therefore, selected neighborhoods with probabilities proportionate to the population in the census tracts as of 1960.

SELECTION OF CONTROL NEIGHBORHOODS, PHASE II

Although the integrated neighborhoods may be used to estimate the totality of integrated neighborhoods in the United States, the same does not apply to the control neighborhoods. A national sample of segregated neighborhoods would differ substantially from the integrated neighborhood sample with respect to geographical location and size of place, types of available housing, and socio-economic status. These large differences would mask the smaller social and psychological factors we attempted to evaluate.

Our control neighborhoods were selected with probabilities proportionate to size after stratifying for the following variables:

1. Primary sampling unit (standard metropolitan area or county);
2. Central city versus remainder of metropolitan area (where applicable);
3. Percentage of single-family housing (50 percent or less, 51–89 percent, 90 percent or more); and
4. Median income (high, medium, or low).

The integrated neighborhoods were divided at random into three equal groups. The first group was used to control the selection of the 53 white segregated control neighborhoods, the second to control the selection of the 53 Negro segregated control neighborhoods, and the third was not used.

The sampling rate for white segregated control neighborhoods varies from stratum to stratum, but it is usually about one-third of the sampling rate for the integrated neighborhoods of similar strata. The sampling rate for Negro segregated control neighborhoods is about 3.3 of the rate for the integrated neighborhoods in the same stratum, or roughly ten times the sampling rate for the white control neighborhoods.

SAMPLING OF INFORMANTS WITHIN NEIGHBORHOODS, PHASE II

Within each neighborhood we conducted a minimum of four interviews with four types of informants who were most likely to be able to give us a complete and reliable picture of their neighborhood: a church informant, a school informant, a community organization informant, and a real estate informant. These informants were not selected at random. For example, our sample of church informants represents the best known and most knowledgeable church leaders and is not merely a random sample of ministers in integrated neighborhoods.

Additional interviews were obtained in a few neighborhoods to settle conflicting reports on the integration status of the neighborhood, or in neighborhoods where one of the informants discussed an area mainly outside the neighborhood boundaries as defined by the other informants. A total of 1,299 interviews with informants were conducted in 311 neighborhoods, and ten additional interviews were discarded because they covered the wrong area.

At the same time that we decided to obtain about 200 integrated neighborhoods, we decided to interview approximately 2,000 white families and 500 Negro families in these neighborhoods. Our overall sampling rate for white families was .0005, or 1 in 2,000. For Negro families, the sampling rate was 2.5 times as large, 1 in 800, or .00125. This was estimated from Phase I of the study, which indicated that the mean proportion of Negroes in a neighborhood is about 10 percent of the population. Since our sample of Negroes was one-fourth of our sample of whites, the sampling rate was 2.5 times larger.

Within each neighborhood, three starting points were selected for listing. Where census block information was available, blocks were chosen with probabilities proportionate to size. Where no block information was available, blocks or other identifiable geographic units were chosen at random with equal probabilities. The sampling rate within blocks for white households was then computed so that

Probability of selection within neighborhood =
Probability of selection of block × Probability
of selection within block

CONTROL NEIGHBORHOOD SAMPLES, PHASE III

The sampling rate within each control neighborhood was selected so that the expected sample would equal that in the corresponding integrated neighborhood. Again, three starting points were selected, and the sampling rate within blocks determined as before.

SPECIAL NEGRO SAMPLE IN OPEN NEIGHBORHOODS,
PHASE III

A rare, but particularly interesting, group are the Negro households in open neighborhoods. Since the number of such households found in using the standard sampling rates is so small, we instructed interviewers to find and interview up to five Negro households in each neighborhood as an additional sample. This resulted in 83 more Negro household interviews. These households are *not* included in any of the tables, except those dealing with Negroes in open and moderately integrated neighborhoods.

MISCLASSIFICATION OF NEIGHBORHOODS AS NEGRO SEGREGATED

We had expected that a small number of neighborhoods would be misclassified by city-wide informants in Phase I, but we thought that the neighborhoods that were initially classified as integrated but turned out to be segregated would balance the neighborhoods that were initially classified as segregated but turned out to be integrated. This was not the case. City-wide informants mistook a substantial number of integrated neighborhoods for Negro segregated neighborhoods. With these mistakes omitted, the remaining misclassifications pretty much cancel each other out.

In retrospect, the city-wide informants' misclassification of integrated as Negro segregated neighborhoods probably reflects the popular misconception that once a Negro family moves into a neighborhood the neighborhood must change.

Although we depended on our neighborhood informants to ultimately classify our neighborhoods as integrated or segregated, we checked their judgments with information from our sample of households. In open neighborhoods we confirmed the presence of Negro residents by conducting interviews with them as a special sample, even if they did not fall into the regular household sample. This prevented the misclassification of white segregated neighborhoods as open neighborhoods.

For substantially integrated neighborhoods, we checked the neighborhood informants' claims that whites were still moving in by looking at the length of time white residents had been in these neighborhoods. In 90 percent of the neighborhoods, there were some white families who had lived in their houses a year or less, indicating that whites were indeed still moving in.

For a neighborhood to be classified as integrated, it was necessary that informants predict no major racial change over the next five years. It is not possible, however, to confirm these predictions of stability without returning to the neighborhoods a few years hence. (We hope to do a second study of these same neighborhoods in 1972.) The rate of change in racial composition is partially indicated by the change between census figures in 1960 and the current estimates. Another indication is given by the proportion of whites and Negroes moving in during the last several years, as estimated from resident information. This indication is subject to very high sampling variability, since only a few residents in a neighborhood moved in during any given year. Except in a few neighborhoods, neither of these indications contradicted the informants' predictions.

CLASSIFICATION OF INTEGRATED NEIGHBORHOODS

Since most of the tables and text in this book differentiate between open, moderately integrated, and substantially integrated neighborhoods, we made strenuous efforts to avoid errors in classification. Our two chief sources of information were the neighborhood informants and the actual results of sampling households in Phase III. In all but forty neighborhoods, the classifications of these two independent sources matched and there was no problem. Where they did not match, we used the following rule:

> If there were more than ten sample households in the neighborhood, the neighborhood was classified using sample results. These sample results are subject to sampling variability for small sample sizes so that in the ten neighborhoods where there were fewer than ten cases in the neighborhood, we took the average of the percentage Negro as estimated by neighborhood informants and averaged that with the percentage Negro as estimated from the sample.

While this procedure does not insure that there are no classification errors, it is unlikely that our analysis is affected by them. Most neighborhoods that were at all uncertain were near the border lines of 1 and 10 percent Negro, so that if a misclassification occurred, the neighborhood was merely shifted to the wrong side of the border.

HOUSEHOLD COOPERATION

Three of four selected respondents cooperated on the household survey phase of this study. This is slightly lower than the cooperation rates generally achieved by NORC on national studies, and is due to the fact that the interviewing assignments were concentrated in the large metropolitan areas of the United States. Past experience has shown that respondents are harder to locate and interview in large cities and their suburbs than in smaller towns or rural areas. The cooperation on this study is, however, roughly comparable to that of other studies in large cities.

The problem of non-response bias must be kept in mind when the reliability of the results is considered. Still the cooperation rate is to a very large extent determined by the population sampled, and not by our field methods. During the field period, which extended from March through July, 1967, at least six call-backs were made on households to find the respondent at home. In case of a refusal, another interviewer was sent to the respondent to try again. There is no indication that the subject matter of the study directly affected the cooperation rate. The respondents who refused were not aware of the nature of the study, and the interviewers did not regard this study as unusually difficult. Most interviewers said that they and the respondents enjoyed the interviews.

References

Abrams, Charles. "The Housing Problem and the Negro." In Talcott Parsons and Kenneth B. Clark (Eds.), *The Negro American*. The Daedalus Library. Houghton Mifflin, 1966.

Bradburn, Norman M. *The Structure of Psychological Well-Being*. Aldine, 1969.

Bradburn, Norman M., and Caplovitz, David. *Reports on Happiness: A Pilot Study of Behavior Related to Mental Health*. Aldine, 1965.

Bradburn, Norman M., Sudman, Seymour, and Gockel, Galen L. *Racial Integration in American Neighborhoods: A Comparative Survey*. Report No. 111-B. National Opinion Research Center, 1970.

Campbell, Angus, and Schuman, Howard. *Racial Attitudes in Fifteen American Cities*, Survey Research Center, University of Michigan, 1968.

Duncan, Otis Dudley. "A Socioeconomic Index for All Occupations." In Albert J. Reiss, Jr., *Occupations and Social Status*. Free Press, 1961.

Grier, Eunice, and Grier, George. *Privately Developed Interracial Housing: An Analysis of Experience*. University of California Press, 1960.

Grier, Eunice, and Grier, George. *Equality and Beyond: Housing Segregation in the Great Society*. Quadrangle Books, 1966.

Jacobs, Jane. *The Death and Life of Great American Cities*. Vintage Books, 1961.

Johnstone, John W. C., and Rivera, Ramon J. *Volunteers for Learning: A Study of the Educational Pursuits of American Adults*. Aldine, 1965.

Laurenti, Luigi. *Property Values and Race: Studies in Seven Cities*. University of California Press, 1961.

Rugaber, Walter. "Housing Equality Hits a Raw Nerve." *The New York Times*, September 20, 1966.

Schwartz, Mildred A. *Trends in White Attitudes Toward Negroes*. Report No. 119. National Opinion Research Center, 1967.

Sudman, Seymour, and Bradburn, Norman M. *Social Psychological Factors in Intergroup Housing: Results of a Pilot Test*. Report No. 111-A. National Opinion Research Center, 1966.

Taeuber, Karl E., and Taeuber, Alma F. *Negroes in Cities: Residential Segregation and Neighborhood Change*. Aldine, 1965.

U.S Bureau of the Census. *Current Population Reports: Consumer Income*. Ser. P-60, No. 53. Government Printing Office, December 28, 1967.

U.S. Commission on Civil Rights. *Housing*. Hearings held in New York, New York (February 2-3, 1959), Atlanta, Georgia (April 10, 1959), and Chicago, Illinois (May 5-6, 1959). Government Printing Office, 1959. Pp. 769-80, 910-11.

Index

Abrams, Charles, 104
Age
—of household head, 89
—of respondent: and interracial sociability in churches, 159
Alinsky, Saul, 79
Attitudes: versus behavior, 118 – 20, 122, 124, 157, 159. *See also* Housing segregation attitudes; Integration attitudes; Negro attitudes.

Block-busting, 64, 71 – 72, 74. 107. *See also* Desegregation, reactions to.
Boswell, James, 99
Bradburn, Norman M., vi, 161n.
Builders, number of, and neighborhood integration, 51, 107

Campbell, Angus, 134
Caplovitz, David, 161n.
Church integration: acceptance of, 156 – 58; extent of, 16, 152 –

53; and interracial sociability, 158 – 59; and location of church attended, 154 – 55; and neighborhood type, 153 – 54; and percent Negro in adjacent neighborhoods, 155 – 56; in profile neighborhoods, 33, 37; and religious affiliation, 16 – 17, 153 – 54, 159; and urbanization, 156
Church location and attendance patterns, 154
Churches: interracial sociability in, 158 – 59; racial composition of, 152 – 56
Cities. *See* Urbanization.
Civil rights activities of Negroes, 14, 130 – 32
Clergymen, activities of, and acceptance of church integration, 158
Commission on Race and Housing, 4
Crime: concern about, 27, 173 – 75, 178; types reported, 175

households, 49, 51; and number of integrated neighborhoods, 49, 51; and ownership status, 108

Socializing, 17, 62; in integrated churches, 158 – 59; and Negro happiness with neighborhood, 164. *See also* Neighboring.

Socio-economic characteristics of households, 13, 87 – 89; and integration attitudes, 122 – 23; and neighborhood type, 88, 90 – 94; for Negroes, 25, 92 – 93; for whites, 90 – 92. *See also* Education; Income, household; Occupation of household head.

Socio-economic variety, 103

Suburbs. *See* Urbanization.

Sudman, Seymour, vi

Taeuber, Alma F., 3, 55

Taeuber, Karl E., 3, 55

Time spent traveling to work, 177

Transportation facilities, availability of, 176 – 77, 178

U.S. Commission on Civil Rights, 79

U.S. Department of Housing and Urban Development, 105

Urban League, 98

Urbanization: and church integration, 156; and concern about crime, 173; and degree of school integration, 138; and general neighboring, 166; and household income, 94; and housing segregation attitudes, 124 – 26; and length of time since desegregation, 69; and number of households, 49, 51, 55 – 56, 63; and number of integrated neighborhoods, 49, 51, 55 – 56; and ownership status, 108 – 9; and religious variety, 102

Variety within neighborhood, 13, 99 – 105; barriers to, 104 – 5; estimates and perceptions of, 100; preference for, 100 – 1, 104; reasons for, 99 – 100. *See also* Homogeneity, preference for; *and individual measures:* Educational variety; Ethnic variety; Income variety; Religious variety.

White exodus, 13, 64, 71 – 72, 74 – 75, 77, 83, 85. *See also* Desegregation, reactions to.

White households, number of, in integrated neighborhoods, 56 – 61

White segregated neighborhoods: distribution of, 190; and integration attitudes, 189 – 90; and Negro housing demand, 189 – 90; possible integration of, 185 – 89; predictions for, 17 – 18, 189 – 91

A NOTE ON THE AUTHORS

Norman M. Bradburn is Director of the National Opinion Research Center and Professor of Behavioral Sciences at the Graduate School of Business of the University of Chicago. Seymour Sudman is Associate Professor of Business Administration and Sociology at the University of Illinois at Urbana Champaign. Galen L. Gockel directs the Urban Studies Program of the Associated Colleges of the Midwest.